my revision notes

Edexcel AS/A-level History

IN SEARCH OF THE AMERICAN DREAM: THE USA

c.1917–96

Alan Farmer

Series editor
Peter Callaghan

HODDER
EDUCATION
AN HACHETTE UK COMPANY

Acknowledgements

The Publishers would like to thank the following for permission to reproduce copyright material.

p.89 *E1*, **p.97** *E1* & **p.100** *E1 The Unfinished Journey*, 5th Edition by Chafe (2003) circa 659w from pp.471–472, 480 © 1986, 1991, 1995 by Oxford University Press, Inc. By permission of Oxford University Press, USA; **p.89** *E2*, **p.91** *E1* & **p.100** *E2* Excerpts from Revolution by Martin Anderson. Published by Hoover Institution Press, Stanford University.

Every effort has been made to trace all copyright holders, but if any have been inadvertently overlooked, the Publishers will be pleased to make the necessary arrangements at the first opportunity.

Although every effort has been made to ensure that website addresses are correct at time of going to press, Hodder Education cannot be held responsible for the content of any website mentioned in this book. It is sometimes possible to find a relocated web page by typing in the address of the home page for a website in the URL window of your browser.

Hachette UK's policy is to use papers that are natural, renewable and recyclable products and made from wood grown in sustainable forests. The logging and manufacturing processes are expected to conform to the environmental regulations of the country of origin.

Orders: please contact Bookpoint Ltd, 130 Milton Park, Abingdon, Oxon OX14 4SE. Telephone: +44 (0)1235 827720. Fax: +44 (0)1235 400401. Email: education@bookpoint.co.uk Lines are open from 9 a.m. to 5 p.m., Monday to Saturday, with a 24-hour message answering service. You can also order through our website: www.hoddereducation.co.uk

ISBN: 978 1 5104 1809 7

First published in 2018 by
Hodder Education,
An Hachette UK Company
Carmelite House
50 Victoria Embankment
London EC4Y 0DZ

www.hoddereducation.co.uk

Impression number   10 9 8 7 6 5 4 3 2

Year   2022 2021 2020 2019 2018

Cover photo © lespalenik/123RF
Illustrations by Integra Software Services
Typeset in Bembo Std Regular 10.75/12.75 by Integra Software Services Pvt. Ltd., Pondicherry, India
Printed in Spain

A catalogue record for this title is available from the British Library.

My Revision Planner

Activity answers and quick quizzes at www.hoddereducation.co.uk/myrevisionnotes

Introduction

About Paper 1

Paper 1 Option 1F: In search of the American Dream: The USA, c.1917–96 requires a breadth of knowledge of a historical period, as well as knowledge of the historical debate around the impact of Reagan's presidency. Paper 1 tests you against two Assessment Objectives: AO1 and AO3.

AO1 tests your ability to:
- organise and communicate your own knowledge
- analyse and evaluate key features of the past
- make supported judgements
- deal with concepts of cause, consequence, change, continuity, similarity, difference and significance.

On Paper 1, AO1 tasks require you to write essays from your own knowledge.

AO3 tests your ability to:
- analyse and evaluate interpretations of the past
- explore interpretations of the past in the context of historical debate.

On Paper 1, the AO3 task requires you to write an essay which analyses the work of historians.

At A-level, Paper 1 is worth 30 per cent of your qualification. At AS Level, Paper 1 is worth 60 per cent of your qualification. Significantly, your AS grade does not count towards your overall A-level grade.

The exam

The Paper 1 AS exam and A-level exam each last for 2 hours and 15 minutes, and are divided into three sections.

Section A and Section B test the breadth of your historical knowledge of the four themes.

Section A requires you to write one essay from a choice of two. Section A questions will usually test your knowledge of at least a decade. You should spend around 35 to 40 minutes on Section A – this includes making a brief plan.

Section B requires you to write one essay from a choice of two. Section B essays usually test your knowledge of a third of the period 1918–79, around 23 years. You should spend around 35 to 40 minutes on Section B – this includes making a brief plan.

Section C tests your knowledge of the debate around the impact of Reagan's presidency on the USA in the years 1981–96. Section C requires you to answer one compulsory question relating to two extracts from the work of historians. Questions will focus on the years 1979–97. You should spend around 35 to 40 minutes on Section C, and an additional 20 minutes to read the extracts and make a plan.

The AS questions are of a lower level in order to differentiate them from the A-level questions. You will find examples of AS and A-level questions throughout the book.

How to use this book

This book has been designed to help you to develop the knowledge and skills necessary to succeed in this exam.
- Each section is made up of a series of topics organised into double-page spreads.
- On the left-hand page, you will find a summary of the key content you need to learn.
- Words in bold in the main content are defined in the glossary.
- On the right-hand page, you will find exam-focused activities.

Together, these two strands of the book will take you through the knowledge and skills essential for examination success.

Examination activities

There are three levels of exam-focused activities.
- Band 1 activities are designed to develop the foundational skills needed to pass the exam. These have a green heading and this symbol.
- Band 2 activities are designed to build on the skills developed in Band 1 activities and to help you achieve a C grade. These have an orange heading and this symbol.
- Band 3 activities are designed to enable you to access the highest grades. These have a purple heading and this symbol.

Each section ends with an exam-style question and model high-level answer with commentary. This should give you guidance on what is required to achieve the top grades.

Activities with this symbol have answers available online.

1 The changing political environment, 1917–80

The rise and decline of Republicanism to 1933

The situation in 1917–21

Woodrow Wilson, a progressive **Democrat**, was re-elected president in 1916 and served a second term from 1917 to 1921. In 1917, Wilson took the USA into the First World War. The end of the war did not leave the USA impoverished and in turmoil as it did much of Europe. Yet it seems to have resulted in a mood of disillusionment. By 1920, Wilsonian zeal, whether for domestic reform or a new world order, was out of fashion. Incapacitated by a stroke in September 1919, Wilson himself proposed no further reform measures during his last two years in office.

The 1920 election

Republican bosses chose Warren Harding, a conservative, as their presidential candidate. The Democrats nominated James Cox. Cox tried to make membership of the **League of Nations** the main campaign issue, but voters were more concerned about rising prices and industrial strife, which they blamed on the party in power. Harding said little about anything. In a typically bland speech, he declared that 'America's present need is not heroics but healing, not nostrums but normalcy.' Whatever 'normalcy' was supposed to mean, it was apparently what Americans wanted. Harding triumphed, winning 61 per cent of the popular vote.

Republican dominance, 1921–29

The Republican Party dominated American politics throughout the 1920s. Sympathetic to big business, the Republicans believed that government intervention in the economy should be kept to a minimum.

Harding declared, 'We want less government in business and more business in government.'

Warren Harding

Harding, an amiable conservative, appointed a number of able men to key posts – for example **Herbert Hoover,** who became secretary of commerce. But Harding gave other posts to some of his 'Ohio Gang'. In 1923, it emerged that there was extensive corruption within his **administration**. Several men, including Interior Secretary Albert Fall, were imprisoned for misappropriating funds or accepting bribes. Harding, not personally implicated in the corruption activities, unexpectedly died in 1923.

Calvin Coolidge

Vice President **Coolidge** now became president. Honest and incorruptible, he did not smoke, drink, play cards or chase women (like Harding). He had a *laissez-faire* philosophy. 'The business of America', he said, 'is business'. In the 1924 election, Coolidge won 15 million votes; John Davis, his Democrat opponent, won 8 million. The USA remained prosperous and Coolidge remained popular, although he did and said very little. To most Americans he became a symbol of traditional values threatened by the forces of change.

The 1928 election

When Coolidge refused to stand in 1928, the Republicans selected Herbert Hoover. An orphaned farm boy, he became a successful mining engineer and was a millionaire before he was 40. Efficient and humanitarian, he was nicknamed 'the wonder boy'. Democrat candidate Al Smith, a Catholic, called for the end of Prohibition. This, and Smith's religion, were the main campaign issues. Hoover won 58 per cent of the popular vote. The Republicans also won large majorities in **Congress**.

Hoover and the Great Depression

Hoover soon faced serious economic problems. In October 1929, the value of stocks and shares plummeted. The **Wall Street** Crash helped bring about the **Great Depression**. By December 1932, 12 million Americans were unemployed. Many blamed Hoover. He was seen as doing too little to improve the economic situation or to help those in need. In reality, he intervened in the economy more energetically than any of his predecessors. He nearly doubled federal public works expenditure in three years. Few politicians advocated more radical measures than those Hoover supported.

The 1932 election

Hoover was re-nominated as Republican presidential candidate. The Democrats chose New York Governor **Franklin D. Roosevelt** (FDR). In July 1932, Roosevelt pledged himself to a **New Deal** for the American people. But he did not define exactly what he intended to do. In November 1932, Roosevelt obtained 22.8 million popular and 472 **Electoral College** votes to Hoover's 15.8 million popular and 59 Electoral College votes. The Democrats also won large majorities in both houses of Congress.

Complete the paragraph   a

Below are a sample exam-style question and a paragraph written in answer to this question. The paragraph contains a point and specific examples, but lacks a concluding analytical link back to the question. Complete the paragraph by adding this link in the space provided.

How accurate is it to say that the American presidents were 'do-nothing presidents' in the period 1921–33?

President Hoover assumed government responsibility for the economic situation after 1930 and intervened in the economy more energetically than any of his predecessors. Few politicians advocated more radical measures than those Hoover supported. Congress, which was controlled by the Democrats after 1930, advocated a balanced budget. It had no real programme except to obstruct Hoover. The Depression seemed to be under control in early 1931. However, as things deteriorated in 1931–32, Hoover was prepared to take direct government action. In 1932, for example, he set up the Reconstruction Finance Corporation to lend money to ailing banks, railroads and insurance companies. Other measures included the Glass-Steagall Banking Act and the Relief and Construction Acts. Hoover nearly doubled federal public works expenditure in three years. Therefore,

_____

_____

_____

! Spot the mistake   a

Below are a sample exam question and a paragraph written in answer to this question. Why does this paragraph not get into Level 4? Once you have identified the mistake, rewrite the paragraph so that it displays the qualities of Level 4. The mark scheme on pages 109–10 will help you.

How far was Republican dominance in American politics the result of the economic situation in the period 1921–28?

The First World War did not leave the USA impoverished and in turmoil, as it did much of Europe. Yet many Americans were concerned by interracial strife, a Red Scare, rising prices and a short-lived repression, all of which they blamed on the Democrats — the party in power. A mood of disillusionment set in. This influenced many aspects of social and political life. Most Americans longed for stability and order.

The influence of Roosevelt

Roosevelt's first term, 1933–36

Inaugurated president in March 1933, Roosevelt remained president for the rest of his life, winning a total of four presidential elections.

Roosevelt's character

In 1921, Roosevelt had been stricken with polio, losing the use of his legs. Remaining cheerful and optimistic, he refused to let this disability end his political career. The complexities of his character baffled contemporaries and still baffle historians. On the one hand, he projected extraordinary charm and warmth. But he could also be evasive and devious. Historian Ted Morgan described him as 'part lion, part fox'.

Roosevelt and the New Deal

In his **inaugural address**, Roosevelt gave Americans hope that he would improve the economic situation. Taking advice from his formal cabinet and his '**Brain Trust**', Roosevelt supported a host of measures to get Americans back to work. One of his strengths was his receptiveness to new ideas. He was also able to 'sell' these ideas to Congress and the public. Projecting a sense of utter self-confidence, he proved himself a masterly politician, reconciling the conflicting views of his reform-minded supporters. By no means were all his New Deal measures successful. But some were and slowly the US economy improved.

The 1936 election

In 1936, Roosevelt was re-nominated on a platform promising more reform. Republican candidate Alfred Landon wanted to reduce public spending and balance the budget. During the bitterly fought campaign, Roosevelt seemed to go out of his way to stir up class hatreds. His strategy worked. He won nearly 61 per cent of the popular vote and carried every state except two. The Democrats totally dominated both houses of Congress.

Roosevelt's second term, 1937–40

FDR's second term was less successful than his first as he had to deal with increased opposition:
- Roosevelt's attempt to reform the **Supreme Court** led to a storm of protest. He was accused of seeking to overthrow the balance of the Constitution.
- Roosevelt's Court plan shattered Democratic unity. It convinced many Democrats (particularly southerners) that Roosevelt had dictatorial ambitions. After 1937, he found it hard to win support in Congress for his measures.

The 1940 election

Roosevelt stood for an unprecedented third time for the presidency in 1940. Given the foreign situation, the USA needed an experienced pair of hands. Helped by the start of a war boom, Roosevelt won almost 55 per cent of the popular vote – 449 Electoral College votes compared to 82 for his Republican opponent Wendell Wilkie.

Roosevelt's third and fourth terms

Roosevelt's last two terms were dominated by the USA's entry into the Second World War in December 1941. Roosevelt proved to be a brilliant war leader. He delegated well and had an excellent grasp of the war's overall direction. Aided by his Chief of Staff Marshall, he made virtually all the right strategic decisions – defeating Germany first, supporting an invasion of France and financing the project that led to the atomic bomb's production.

The 1944 election

In November 1944, Roosevelt won his fourth presidential election. He did so with fewer votes than in 1940 – a sign that opinion was moving to the right.

Roosevelt's death

In April 1945, Roosevelt died suddenly. He had served the USA at a crucial time. Virtually everything he tried to do sparked controversy. The twentieth century's most loved and most hated president, he was also probably its best. Roosevelt was, in British Prime Minister Winston Churchill's view, 'the greatest man I have ever known'.

Support or challenge?

Below is a sample exam-style question which asks you to what extent you agree with a specific statement. Below that is a list of general statements which are relevant to the question. Using your own knowledge and the information on the opposite page, decide whether these statements support or challenge the statement in question.

How far do you agree that Roosevelt united Americans during the course of his presidencies in the years 1933–41?

Statement	Support	Challenge
Roosevelt won an overwhelming majority in the 1932 election.		
Roosevelt's New Deal measures did not win universal support.		
Roosevelt easily won the 1936 election.		
Roosevelt lost support as a result of his challenge to the Supreme Court.		
Many Southern Democrats opposed Roosevelt after 1937.		
Roosevelt won a convincing victory in the 1940 election.		
The economic situation helped Roosevelt in 1940.		

 Identify key terms

Below is a sample exam question which includes a key word or term. Key terms are important because their meaning can be helpful in structuring your answer, developing an argument and establishing criteria that will help form the basis of a judgement.

How accurate is it so say that Roosevelt's presidency went from strength to strength in the years 1933–1945?

- First, identify the key word or term. This will be a word or phrase that is important to the meaning of the question. Underline the word or phrase.
- Secondly, define the key phrase. Your definition should set out the key features of the phrase or word that you are defining.
- Third, make an essay plan that reflects your definition.
- Finally, write a sentence answering the question that refers back to the definition.

Now repeat the task, and consider how the change in key terms affects the structure, argument and final judgement of your essay.

To what extent was Roosevelt a more successful wartime than peacetime president?

Changing styles of presidential leadership, 1945–72 REVISED

American presidents have invariably had different styles of leadership. This was evident in the years from 1945 to 1972.

Harry Truman, 1945–52

Vice President **Truman** became president after Roosevelt's death. Having little previous governmental experience, Truman had to learn fast. He quickly grew in confidence and proved himself a determined and decisive president who was prepared to take strong action – not least the decision to drop atomic bombs on Hiroshima and Nagasaki in 1945. After victory in the Second World War, he committed the USA to standing firm against the **USSR**. To most pundits' surprise, Truman won the 1948 election after a barnstorming tour across America. In 1950, he went to war to save South Korea from **Communist** aggression. At home, Truman's efforts to end racial discrimination had only limited success.

Dwight D. Eisenhower, 1953–61

Eisenhower had a successful career in the US army, commanding the victorious Allied armies in Europe in 1944–45. His ability to foster teamwork and confidence was particularly impressive. In 1952, he won the Republican nomination and defeated Democrat Adlai Stevenson with 55 per cent of the vote. Given that the USA was still at war in Korea, he seemed – and was – a safe (conservative) pair of hands. Re-elected president in 1956, he exuded calmness and strength. His ill health was a problem but most Americans trusted and liked 'Ike'.

John F. Kennedy, 1961–63

Kennedy (JFK), the Democrat candidate, defeated **Richard Nixon,** Eisenhower's vice president, in a closely fought election in 1960. Handsome and charismatic, Kennedy was in many ways the first television-generated president. Determined to stand up to the USSR, he took the world to the brink of nuclear war during the **Cuban Missile Crisis** in 1962. Kennedy was less liberal on domestic matters than many thought. Nevertheless, by 1963 he was committed to the cause of civil rights. President for only a thousand days, he was assassinated in Dallas in November 1963. His untimely death gave him something of a heroic status, which may be undeserved. With Kennedy, style often outweighed substance.

Lyndon Baines Johnson, 1963–69

Vice President **Johnson** (LBJ) became president on Kennedy' death. A tough, experienced liberal politician, Johnson used Kennedy's death to push a wide-ranging Civil Rights Bill through Congress. In 1964, he decisively defeated Republican Barry Goldwater, polling 61 per cent of the total votes. In 1965 Johnson supported the **Great Society** programme, committing his administration to a war on poverty, racial equality, educational reform and improvement in housing. Not all his measures were successful but his civil rights legislation and **Medicare** helped improve many lives. After 1965 he massively escalated US involvement in the Vietnam War (despite promises in the 1964 election that he would not do so). His presidency was increasingly accompanied by anti-war and other protests. Blamed by many Americans for the tumult on the streets, Johnson was so unpopular he decided not to stand for re-election in 1968.

Richard Nixon's first term, 1968–72

Nixon, the Republican candidate, defeated Democrat Hubert Humphrey, in 1968 – an election in which right-wing Southerner George Wallace won 13.5 per cent of the total vote as an independent candidate. Nixon was a pragmatic politician. Once associated with his party's right wing, by 1968 he was seen – and saw himself – as a moderate. He prided himself on representing the views of Middle America. He also sought to win the support of white Southerners who no longer felt at home in the liberal Democrat party. Nixon was not generally liked or trusted. But he slowly de-escalated the Vietnam War and improved relations with the USSR and China. He was less successful in dealing with the USA's growing economic problems. Nevertheless, in 1972, standing against liberal Democrat George McGovern, Nixon won 60.7 per cent of the vote – 520 electoral votes to only 17 for McGovern. During the course of the campaign, McGovern complained about the 'dirty tricks' of the Republicans, not least the fact that a group of burglars were caught breaking into the Democratic National Committee headquarters in the Watergate complex in Washington (see page 12).

Simple essay style

Below is a sample exam question. Use your own knowledge and the information on the opposite page to produce a plan for this question. Choose four general points, and provide three pieces of specific information to support each general point. Once you have planned your essay, write the introduction and conclusion for the essay. The introduction should list the points to be discussed in the essay. The conclusion should summarise the key points and justify which point was the most important.

To what extent was Eisenhower the USA's most successful president in the years 1945–72?

 Eliminate irrelevance

Below are a sample exam question and a paragraph written in answer to this question. Read the paragraph and identify parts of the paragraph that are not directly relevant to the question. Draw a line through the information that is irrelevant and justify your decision in the margin.

To what extent were American presidents generally trusted and respected by the electorate in the years 1945–72?

By 1968, Richard Nixon had abandoned his earlier divisiveness. He now portrayed himself as the candidate of peace and national harmony. Having defeated Hubert Humphrey in the very close 1968 election, Nixon set about trying to bring Americans together. He had some success. He managed to withdraw huge numbers of US troops from Vietnam without losing the war and he also improved relations with China and Russia. His domestic policies were less successful, particularly on the economic front. In 1971, with inflation and unemployment rising, he abruptly abandoned his hostility to economic controls and ordered a ninety-day freeze on wages, prices and rents and called for a tax cut to stimulate the dollar. The general thrust of his domestic policy was conservative. Appealing to the spirit of individualism, he undermined and dismantled many of Johnson's social welfare programmes and vetoed much new health, education and welfare legislation emanating from a Democratic-controlled Congress. Many Americans did not trust 'Tricky Dicky'. Nevertheless, the 'silent majority' seemed to respect him. This was shown in the 1972 presidential election when he won an overwhelming victory over George McGovern, a liberal senator from South Dakota. Nixon won nearly 61 per cent of the popular vote, a larger share than any previous candidate except Lyndon Johnson in 1964. But Nixon was soon to lose the respect he had built up in his first term. In his second term he was soon embroiled in the Watergate scandal. Nixon denied all knowledge of the break-in at the Democratic party headquarters in the Watergate apartment building in Washington. But it soon emerged that some of Nixon's closest White House associates had planned the break-in and had subsequently conspired with others to cover up their involvement. As the affair dragged on, Senate investigators uncovered evidence of one presidential misdeed after another and most Americans lost confidence in their president. In 1974, he resigned the presidency rather than face impeachment charges.

A decline in confidence, 1968–80

US problems, 1968–72

By 1968, the USA faced a number of problems. These included:

- the continuing Vietnam War, which the USA was clearly not winning.
- divisions at home between black and white, young and old, rich and poor.
- economic problems, including rising inflation and growing unemployment.

Americans lost confidence in Johnson because he was seen as responsible for these problems. Nor did they have much confidence in Nixon. Although Nixon won a landslide victory in 1972, he was not particularly popular. Unfortunately for Nixon, the elections left the Democrats in control of Congress.

Watergate

Nixon's second term was dominated by the Watergate scandal. Watergate resulted from men breaking into the Democrat Party headquarters in the course of the 1972 election in an attempt to discover Democrat plans. As investigations developed, it became increasingly clear that Nixon had lied about his role in the break-in and had tried to obstruct justice. In 1974, Nixon chose to resign rather than face an **impeachment** trial.

The impact of Watergate

- The scandal, which was hardly a good advertisement for democracy, led to a decline in America's international standing.
- It is sometimes seen as the end of the **imperial presidency**.
- It contributed to increased popular cynicism towards – and distrust of – politicians and government.

Ford's presidency, 1974–77

Gerald Ford had become vice president after Spiro Agnew's resignation (as a result of another scandal). He remains the only American president not elected as president or vice president. Ford, who lost some popular support after he pardoned Nixon, proved an easy target for liberal media coverage because of his gaffes and 'falls', whether on ski slopes or down plane ramps. Perhaps this led to decreased respect for the presidency. However, Ford did help restore stability after Watergate. He declared on 4 July 1976: 'I guess we've healed America'.

The 1976 election

In 1976 Ford stood against Southern Democrat **Jimmy Carter.** Neither candidate aroused much enthusiasm. Polled on whether the candidates had presidential quality, over 75 per cent of Americans thought both Ford and Carter lacked it. The result was the lowest presidential election turnout since 1948: only 54 per cent of eligible Americans voted. Carter won 49.9 per cent of the vote, Ford 47.9 per cent.

Carter's presidency, 1977–81

Carter did not re-establish faith in the presidency.

The loss of national self-confidence

In the late 1970s, the USA seemed to be a nation in crisis.

- The economy continued to suffer from inflation (mostly due to rising oil prices and government over-spending), a **balance of trade deficit** and unemployment.
- The USSR seemed to be winning the **Cold War**.
- Carter did not handle the 1979 **Iran hostage crisis** effectively.
- Carter's administration was involved in a number of scandals, one involving his brother Billy who admitted receiving a 'loan' from the Libyan government.

The 1980 election

In 1980, Carter stood against Republican **Ronald Reagan.** Many voters were dissatisfied with Carter's apparent lack of leadership. Reagan, a former actor, inspired far more confidence. In a television debate with Carter, he asked Americans whether they felt anything was better after four years of Carter's presidency. Reagan won the election convincingly, securing 51% of the popular vote to Carter's 41%. However, only 53% of the electorate turned out to vote, suggesting disillusionment with politics in general. By 1980, fewer Americans believed in the **American dream** or thought it had been achieved.

Develop the detail

a

Below are a sample exam-style question and a paragraph written in answer to the question. The paragraph contains a limited amount of detail. Annotate the paragraph to add additional detail to the answer.

How far was Richard Nixon responsible for bringing the American presidency into disrepute in the years 1969–74?

> In 1973, Nixon tried to prevent the release of White House tapes. One tape proved that Nixon had ordered the cover-up and engaged in a conspiracy to obstruct justice. Congress now began the process of impeachment. Aware that he was likely to be found guilty, Nixon resigned.

Turning assertion into argument

Below are a sample exam-style question and a series of assertions. Read the exam question and then add a justification to each of the assertions to turn it into an argument.

To what extent did American presidents bring the presidency into disrepute in the years 1968–80?

Johnson helped bring the presidency into disrepute because…

_____

_____

Watergate was a disaster for the USA because…

_____

_____

Ford did not inspire confidence because…

_____

_____

Jimmy Carter was seen as an ineffective president because…

_____

_____

From 'rugged individualism' to New Deal ideas, 1920s–30s

Rugged individualism

In the 1920s, many Americans accepted the notion of 'rugged individualism' – the belief that government intervention in the economy should be kept to a minimum.

Big business

For most of the 1920s, America – albeit by no means all Americans – basked in unparalleled prosperity. Many Americans attributed their success to big business. President Harding declared 'We want less government in business and more business in government.' President Coolidge's victory in 1924 led to an extension of pro-business policies – low taxation and frugal government expenditure.

The impact of the Great Depression

Mass unemployment after 1929 brought fear and despair. There was no welfare payments system and private charity was unable to cope with the scale of the emergency. Thus there were demands for government intervention to create jobs and to help those in need.

President Hoover's reaction

Although a supporter of 'rugged individualism', Hoover intervened in the economy more energetically than any of his predecessors.

- He stepped up federal spending on roads, bridges and public buildings.
- He set up the Federal Farm Board to bolster farm prices.
- He created the Reconstruction Finance Corporation to lend money to ailing banks, railroads and insurance companies.
- The 1932 federal budget ended up $2.7 billion in the red – the largest peacetime deficit in US history.

Given that there were 13 million Americans unemployed in 1932, Hoover's critics claimed he did not do enough.

The New Deal

In 1932, Roosevelt pledged himself to a New Deal for the American people. He also promised 'bold, persistent experimentation'. However, it was far from clear what his exact intentions were.

Roosevelt's aims

Roosevelt's main concern was to get the USA on the road to recovery. Convinced that the government must lead the recovery, he presided over an administration which was more interventionist and directive than Hoover's. While his programmes soon involved an unprecedented amount of national economic planning, the charge that he sought to introduce socialism were absurd. He intended to save, not destroy, US capitalism.

Roosevelt's actions

In the first hundred days of his presidency, Roosevelt took unprecedented action. The Democrat-controlled Congress, glad to be given a lead by the president, passed 15 major bills affecting unemployment, relief, industry, agriculture, banking, transport and the currency. This body of legislation, unparalleled in scope and volume as well as the speed with which it was enacted, was full of contradiction and overlap. There were some well-considered moves but much was knee-jerk reaction. But at least Roosevelt was doing something.

The Second New Deal

Roosevelt introduced another spate of measures in 1935. These measures, more sweeping than his earlier legislation, shaped the USA for the next half-century. They included the creation of the Works Progress Administration, the Social Security Act, a new Wealth Tax and the National Labour Relations Act.

Was the New Deal new?

The New Deal is often seen as a dramatic change in the USA's history, perhaps even the '**third American Revolution**'. Arguably, Roosevelt founded the modern American welfare state, reduced the autonomy of individual states and transformed the institution of the presidency, making it the chief policy-maker and the focus of Americans' hopes and expectations. However, it is also possible to claim that the New Deal was, at best, a half-way revolution.

- The New Deal did not challenge the basic tenets of capitalism.
- Much of Roosevelt's policy echoed that of Woodrow Wilson and Herbert Hoover.
- The New Deal did not redistribute national income to any extent.
- Roosevelt, reluctant to engage in massive deficit spending, hankered after balancing the budget.

Spectrum of importance

Below are a sample exam question and a list of general points, which could be used to answer the question. Use your own knowledge and the information on the opposite page to reach a judgement about the importance of these general points to the question posed. Write numbers on the spectrum below to indicate their relative importance. Having done this, write a brief justification of your placement, explaining why some of these factors are more important than others. The resulting diagram could form the basis of an essay plan.

How accurate is to say that the New Deal was 'America's third Revolution' in the years 1933–37?

1 Rugged individualism in the 1920s

2 The impact of the Great Depression

3 Hoover's actions 1929–33

4 The 1932 election

5 Roosevelt's aims in 1933

6 The Hundred Days

7 The Second New Deal

8 The 1936 election

9 The situation by 1937

←——————————————————————————————————————→

Least important   Most important

Developing an argument

Below are a sample exam-style question, a list of key points to be made in the essay and a paragraph from the essay. Read the question, the plan and the sample paragraph. Rewrite the paragraph in order to develop an argument. Your paragraph should explain why the factor discussed in the paragraph is linked to the question. Crucially, it should develop an argument by setting out a general answer to the question and reasons that support this.

How far do you agree that the nature of government under Roosevelt was radically different from government under Hoover in the years 1929–37?

Key points

- Hoover basically supported rugged individualism.
- Hoover did something after 1929 – but not enough.
- Roosevelt was committed to federal intervention in economic matters.
- Roosevelt did far more than Hoover.

President Hoover did not take much action to put the USA on the road to recovery. Most of his measures depended for success on the voluntary action of others — of state governments in maintaining spending, of farmers in reducing production, of employers in sustaining wages, of bankers in extending credit. Hoover saw unemployment relief as a matter for private charity and state and local — but not federal — government. He thought that a federal relief programme would unbalance the budget, create a permanent class of dependents, deprive individuals of a sense of responsibility and destroy the nation's moral fibre.

The Red Scares and anti-Communism, 1917–80

The Red Scare of 1919

The 1917 Russian Revolution aroused fears of Communism (associated with the colour red, hence the 'Red Scare'). Americans were alarmed at the emergence of an American Communist movement, largely foreign-born in membership. A wave of industrial unrest in 1919 was widely interpreted as revolutionary. Fear of revolution increased when home-made bombs were posted to politicians and industrialists. An **anarchist** bomb killed 38 people on Wall Street.

Reaction

A wave of repression followed.

● Congress expelled socialist members.

● Thirty-two states passed laws making membership of **syndicalist** organisations a crime.

● Around 9,000 people were arrested and held without trial: over 500 aliens were deported.

The growth of anti-Communism

Fear of Communism existed throughout the inter-war period. After 1945, as the Cold War developed, many Americans feared Communist infiltration.

Truman's actions

Communist spies, searching for atomic secrets, had infiltrated several government agencies. There was also concern that there were Communists within the film industry and education. In 1947 Truman:

● established a Loyalty Review Board to investigate all federal employees

● allowed the **FBI** to investigate subversives.

And by 1950:

● Republican politicians, like Nixon, realised that anti-Communism was an issue that was likely to win themselves and their party support.

● The Korean War broke out in 1950, creating conditions in which anti-Communism bred.

McCarthyism

Efforts to root out Communists became associated with Senator Joseph McCarthy of Wisconsin.

McCarthy's rise

In 1950, McCarthy claimed he had evidence that 205 Communists had infiltrated the State Department. Many veteran anti-Communists, like FBI Director J. Edgar Hoover, were surprised at how little McCarthy actually knew. But through a monumental bluff, McCarthy placed himself at the centre of the anti-Communist movement. Over the next two years he attacked government agencies, the Democratic Party, intellectual liberals and Truman himself. To many Americans, especially blue-collar workers who usually voted Democrat, McCarthy seemed a heroic crusader. He also won the support of other Republican politicians, J. Edgar Hoover and several leading newspapers.

The 1952 election

In the 1952 election, the main issues were the three 'K's – Korea, Communism and corruption. Republican presidential candidate Eisenhower disliked McCarthy. Nevertheless, he used his vice presidential candidate Nixon to beat the anti-Communist drum. The Communist issue helped Eisenhower win the election.

McCarthy's fall

McCarthy's '**witch hunt**' was at its height in 1953–54. He conducted widely publicised hearings into subversive infiltration. In 1954, investigations into the army were broadcast on television. McCarthy was exposed as a brutish and malicious individual, so much so that the **Senate** passed a motion of censure on him. He immediately fell from grace, losing his influence. Nevertheless, anti-Communism remained a force in the USA until the 1980s. Many Americans, in the 1960s, for example, regarded civil rights activism and other protest movements as Communist-driven.

The age of fear?

The period of 1945–54 has been labelled the 'age of fear':

● Conservatives feared that Communists posed a threat externally and internally. They were concerned that Communists had infiltrated the US government.

● Liberals feared that America's traditional freedoms were being eroded by witch hunts. They were appalled that hundreds of teachers and government workers, suspected of being Communist sympathisers, had lost their jobs.

In reality, both sets of fears were exaggerated:

● While Communist agents did exist, very few held positions where they had access to important information or could influence US policy.

● **McCarthyism** did result in lost jobs and books being removed from library shelves. But there were no executions, no **lynchings**, no prison camps and no threat to democratic government.

Delete as applicable

Below are a sample exam question and an introduction written in answer to this question. Read the paragraph and decide which of the possible options (in bold) is most appropriate. Delete the least appropriate options and complete the paragraph by justifying your selection.

How far do you agree that the anti-Communist witch hunts were a threat to the USA's traditional freedoms in the years 1945–54?

Between 1945 and 1954 the USA saw a strong anti-Communist movement emerge. This movement, usually associated with Senator Joseph McCarthy, posed a **severe/moderate/minor** threat to America's traditional freedoms of speech and thought. Many Americans believed that Communism posed a greater threat. The Communist threat loomed large abroad, especially in Europe (from the USSR) and in Asia (from China). The fear that the American government had been infiltrated by Communist agents and sympathisers was a real one. But was the action taken against fellow Americans justified? This essay will argue that the witch hunts were a **severe/moderate/minor** threat because

_____

_____

Simple essay style

Below is a sample exam question. Use your own knowledge and the information on the opposite page to produce a plan for this question. Choose four general points, and provide three pieces of specific information to support each general point. Once you have planned your essay, write the introduction and conclusion for the essay. The introduction should list the points to be discussed in the essay. The conclusion should summarise the key points and justify which point was the most important.

How accurate is it to say that Senator McCarthy was wrong in detail but right in essentials in his efforts to expose Communist infiltrators in the years 1950–54?

Liberalism, counterculture and the conservative reaction, c1960–80

Liberalism in the 1960s

In the 1960s many Americans, especially the young, became increasingly liberal. Liberals supported a number of views:

- Most supported the Civil Rights movement.
- Most opposed the Vietnam War.
- Most wanted the government to help poor Americans.
- Some favoured experimentation, including sexual liberation, drug-taking and alternative lifestyles.

Johnson's presidency

Johnson sympathised with some but not all of the liberal causes.

- He supported civil rights (see page 28).
- He wanted to create a Great Society (see page 76).

But Johnson was at odds with liberals with regard to:
- the Vietnam War
- counter-cultural movements, for which he had little sympathy.

Counter-cultural movements

There is disagreement over the definition of 'counterculture'. Some define it as including all who protested against the dominant culture, such as feminists, anti-war activists and hippies. Others focus solely on hippies.

Hippies

Hippies rejected American society's emphasis on individualism, competitiveness and materialism. Instead, they espoused communal living and harmony. In the mid-1960s, a group of alienated young people moved into San Francisco's Haight-Ashbury area, wearing alternative clothes, smoking and selling cannabis and growing their hair. The greatest counterculture happening was the Woodstock rock festival in 1969, which 400,000 people attended. By the mid-1970s, the hippie movement had faded. It had drawn attention to health foods, environmentalism and Eastern philosophy, and contributed to the liberalisation of attitudes to drugs and sex. Overall, however, its impact was less than that of those who protested against the Vietnam War and racial and gender inequality.

The role of the media

The media, especially television, provided exhaustive coverage of the protest movements and counterculture of the 1960s. Making much of the unusual, it gave the hippies and the Black Panthers coverage out of all proportion to the numbers involved.

Reaction to counterculture

The counter-cultural movements and mass protests of 1968 triggered a conservative reaction.

Nixon's election, 1968

By 1968, many Americans had lost patience with rioters and with a federal government they perceived as taxing them to give the money away to the undeserving poor. In the 1968 election, Republican candidate Nixon appealed to the non-young, non-poor and non-black, to the middle-aged, middle-class and middle-minded: in other words, to all those who opposed 1960s radicalism, change and disorder. This 'silent majority' voted Nixon into power (just) in 1968 and overwhelmingly in 1972.

Bringing America together

Nixon hoped to bring the American people together. This was no easy matter. His inauguration was marred by anti-war protesters. The protests continued.

- In October–November 1969, huge anti-war protests occurred across America.
- When Nixon appeared to be extending the Vietnam War to Cambodia in 1970, anti-war protests erupted in most American universities.
- Nixon also faced pro-civil rights, pro-Black Panther and anti-capitalist protests.

Nixon successfully decreased the number of protests by:
- withdrawing troops from Vietnam
- ordering FBI surveillance of disruptive groups
- threatening to end federal scholarships and loans for student trouble-makers.

Evangelical Christians

- The Catholic Church opposed abortion, setting up the National Right to Life Committee in 1967. This had considerable support, holding mass rallies.
- The Religious Right was increasingly influential in the 1970s. Its supporters espoused traditional values opposing feminism, divorce, drug-taking, pre-marital sex and homosexuality.
- An estimated 5 million evangelical Christians who had not previously voted, voted for Reagan in 1980.

Mind map

Use the information on the opposite page to add detail (at least two points) to the mind map below.

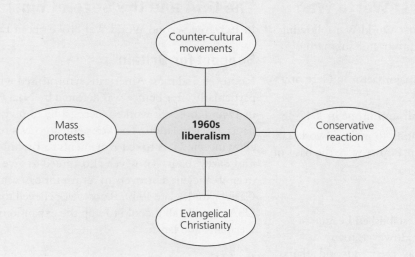

 Develop the detail　**a**

Below are a sample exam-style question and a paragraph written in answer to this question. The paragraph contains a limited amount of detail. Annotate the paragraph to add additional detail to the answer.

How successful was the Hippie movement in the years 1960–80?

The Hippie movement was essentially a youth movement. Hippies aimed to challenge traditional American culture and values. They opposed materialism and supported communal living. They preferred to 'make love, not war'. They wore alternative clothes and liked to experiment by taking drugs.

The return to normalcy and support for isolationism, 1917–41

The impact of the First World War

In 1917, the USA entered the First World War following Germany's re-introduction of unrestricted submarine warfare. This led to:

● a boost to Allied morale – a major factor in Germany's defeat in 1918

● some 100,000 American deaths in Europe in 1917–18

● President Wilson's determination to make a 'world safe for democracy'. His **Fourteen Points** were the basis of the Treaty of Versailles (1919).

The League of Nations

Wilson hoped that the recently established League of Nations would maintain peace. However, many Americans, opposed to US involvement in world affairs, had no wish to join the League. When Wilson refused to accept some Republican amendments to the League, the Senate refused to ratify the Versailles Treaty.

The return to normalcy

In 1920, Democrat presidential candidate James Cox tried to make US membership of the League the main campaign issue. However, voters supported Republican Warren Harding, who promised a return to 'normalcy'. Whatever 'normalcy' was supposed to mean, it was apparently what Americans wanted. Harding won 61 per cent of the vote. Consequently, the USA did not join the League. Instead, Americans drew back into **isolationism**.

American isolationism, 1920–39

During the 1920s and 30s, Americans were wary of getting involved in international affairs.

● Americans became convinced that arms manufacturers and international bankers had 'persuaded' Congressmen and public opinion to support US entry into the First World War.

● After 1929, most Americans were preoccupied with the economic consequences of the Great Depression.

● Roosevelt favoured US participation in the international community. But opinion in Congress tied his hands.

● In 1935, Congress passed the first Neutrality Act which required the President to put an impartial arms embargo on all belligerents. A second Neutrality Act (1936) added a ban on loans to belligerents.

The USA and the Second World War

In 1939, the Second World War broke out in Europe.

Support for Britain

Roosevelt and most Americans sympathised with Britain, particularly after France was defeated by Nazi Germany in 1940. Roosevelt worked successfully to revise neutrality legislation. The arms embargo was repealed, allowing the USA to sell armaments to Britain on a '**cash and carry**' basis. Roosevelt also agreed to give Britain over 40 ancient destroyers in return for bases in the Caribbean. By late 1940, Roosevelt believed that the USA must do all it could to stop the expansionist powers Germany and Japan.

Isolationism

Isolationism remained a powerful belief. The America First movement, which campaigned against US involvement in war, had millions of supporters.

The 1940 election

US involvement in the war was a major issue in the 1940 election. In order to defeat Republican Wendell Wilkie, Roosevelt assured Americans, 'Your boys are not going to be sent into any foreign wars'. Assisted by the start of an economic boom (resulting from the European war), Roosevelt won 55 per cent of the vote.

Increasing US involvement

● In December 1940, Roosevelt told Americans that the USA must become 'the arsenal of democracy'.

● In 1941, Roosevelt persuaded Congress to support **lend-lease** aid to Britain worth $7 billion.

● By autumn 1941, the USA was involved in an undeclared war against German U-boats in the Atlantic.

● US economic actions against Japan led to Japanese retaliation. On 7 December 1941, Japanese planes bombed the US Pacific Fleet at Pearl Harbor. The USA now declared war on Japan.

● On 11 December 1941, Hitler declared war on the USA.

Spot the mistake a

Below are a sample exam question and a paragraph written in answer to this question. Why does the paragraph not get into Level 4? Once you have identified the mistake, rewrite the paragraph so that it displays the qualities of Level 4. The mark scheme on pages 109–10 will help you.

How successful was American foreign policy in the years 1933–41?

> American isolationist policies in the 1930s allowed the expansionist powers of Germany, Italy and Japan to increase their strength. These non-democratic powers were a potential threat to the USA. Isolationism, albeit popular, was a far from successful policy.

 Introducing an argument

Below are an exam question, an essay plan and a basic introduction and conclusion. Rewrite the introduction and conclusion so that they contain an argument about the USA's commitment to isolationism between 1917 and 1941.

To what extent was America committed to isolationism in the years 1917–41?

Key points
- The USA committed itself to the First World War in 1917.
- It initially committed itself to preserving peace after 1918.
- Americans preferred isolationism to international involvement from 1920–39.
- By 1940–41, Roosevelt and most Americans were committed to supporting Britain.

Introduction

> The USA joined the First World War in 1917, following Germany's re-introduction of unrestricted submarine war. President Wilson hoped to ensure that after Germany's defeat the world would become a safer place for democracy. Americans did not share his commitment to international involvement. From 1920–39, most supported isolationism. In 1940–41, faced with the prospect of German and Japanese expansionism, most Americans supported Roosevelt's support for Britain.

Conclusion

> In conclusion, the USA was committed to isolationism for most of the period 1917–41. The only exception was 1917–19 and 1939–41.

The USA's emergence as a Cold War superpower, 1941–50 `REVISED` ☐

The impact of the Second World War

The USA had a major impact on the Second World War. The war also had an enormous impact on the USA.

The US economy

By 1945, the USA produced 45 per cent of the world's arms, built two-thirds of all the world's ships and made half of all the world's goods. America prospered during the war. US cities did not suffer bomb damage. There was full employment and workers, including many women, were well paid.

The political situation

During the war the American electorate swung to the right. Roosevelt won the 1944 election but not by a convincing majority. By 1946, the Republican Party controlled both Houses of Congress.

The situation in 1945

- The USA had suffered 292,000 deaths.
- It had mobilised over 12 million men.
- The USA had paid the least of all the major Allies in lives. It had also avoided being bombed or invaded.
- The USA emerged as the world's wealthiest and strongest power. It was the only country to have atomic weapons, which it used to bring the war with Japan to an end by bombing Hiroshima and Nagasaki.

The start of the Cold War

It was not clear exactly what role the USA would play on the world stage after 1945.

The Truman Doctrine

Some Americans wished to return to isolationism. Many were not convinced of the reality and magnitude of the Soviet threat. However, most politicians soon accepted that the USSR was a danger. In March 1947, President Truman declared 'I believe that it must be the policy of the United States to support free peoples who are resisting attempted subjugation by armed minorities or by outside pressures.' The Truman Doctrine was to be the guiding spirit of US foreign policy for the next half-century. In May 1947, Congress gave $400,000,000 to Greece and Turkey to help ensure they did not fall to Communism.

Marshall Aid

In June 1947, US Secretary of State George Marshall offered US economic assistance to Europe, the countries of which were suffering from poverty and chaos. The aim of Marshall Aid was threefold:

- to help Europeans
- to promote Europe economically so that Europeans would buy American goods
- to stop a poverty-struck Europe adopting Communism.

The CIA

In 1947, the Central Intelligence Agency (**CIA**) was created. In 1948, it was given authority to mount covert operations against Communists.

The situation in the USA

While some Republicans opposed the cost of Marshall Aid, most Americans supported it. They also supported the Truman Doctrine and the formation of the CIA. Soviet actions in 1947–48 seemed akin to Hitler's in 1938–39. Most Americans agreed with Truman that Stalin had to be deterred, not appeased. Many feared that the US government had been infiltrated by Communist spies and sympathisers.

The 1948 election

Against the predictions of most political reporters, Truman won the 1948 presidential election. His victory was probably due to the economic feel-good factor. But Truman's success also suggests that most Americans supported his tough stance against Communism both abroad and at home (see page 16).

The situation in 1948–50

The USA took on a world policeman's role in its effort to contain Communism. The USA was successful in Europe.

- In September 1948, the USSR blockaded West Berlin. Truman stood firm, organising a massive air lift to provide Berliners with 13,000 tons of goods per day. Stalin lifted the blockade in May 1949.
- In April 1949, the **NATO** alliance was formed.

The USA was less successful in Asia. The loss of China to the Communists in 1949 was a serious setback, damaging Truman's reputation as a Cold War warrior. To many Americans, China's loss was evidence that the State Department and other government agencies were riddled with Communist spies. The fact that the USSR exploded its own atomic bomb in 1949 seemed – indeed was – proof that there were spies in the USA's atomic programme.

Establish criteria

Below is a sample exam-style question which requires you to make a judgement. The key term in the question has been underlined. Defining the meaning of the key term can help you establish criteria that you can use to make a judgement.

Read the question, define the key term and then set out two or three criteria based on the key term, which you can use to reach and justify a judgement.

How accurate is it to say that most Americans supported President Truman's Cold War policies in the years 1945–50?

Definition:

_____

_____

_____

Criteria to judge the extent to which Americans supported Truman's Cold War policies in the years 1945–50:

_____

_____

_____

_____

Reach a judgement

Having defined the key term and established a series of criteria, you should now make a judgement. Consider how far Americans supported Truman's Cold War policies according to each criterion. Summarise your judgements below:

Criterion 1:

_____

Criterion 2:

_____

Criterion 3:

_____

Criterion 4:

_____

Finally, sum up your judgement. Based on the criteria, how accurate is it to say that Americans supported Truman's Cold War policies in the years 1945–50?

_____

_____

_____

_____

The impact of involvement in Korea and Vietnam

The Korean War

In 1950–53, the USA successfully defended South Korea from North Korean and Chinese aggression. Around 33,000 Americans died.

The domestic impact

Most Americans believed that the Communists were the aggressors and that the USA and its allies were fighting a 'just war'. While President Truman took the US into conflict, the war led to many Americans supporting the Republicans. McCarthyism (see page 16) was at its height during the Korean War.

The 1952 election

Republican candidate Eisenhower benefited politically from the Korean War. A Second World War hero, he seemed the right man to lead the nation. He declared during the campaign that he would go to Korea, implying that he would end the war. The war did end shortly after Eisenhower came to power, in part because Chinese leaders feared he might use nuclear weapons. The fact that he secured peace meant his presidency got off to a good start.

The Vietnam War

If the Korean War was generally perceived to be a 'good' war, the Vietnam War (1963–73) came increasingly to be seen as a 'bad' war. The USA lost the war and 56,000 dead.

Escalation and growing opposition

President Kennedy took the US into Vietnam. However, it was Johnson who escalated the war. By 1968 there were 538,000 service personnel in South Vietnam. Johnson had to introduce the draft to ensure he had sufficient forces.

Initially, most Americans supported the war. But as more Americans died, opposition grew. Television coverage of the war did not help the American cause. Night after night, reporters brought the suffering, destruction and horror of war into American living rooms. By 1967, there was a growing anti-war movement, especially among students. Between January–June 1968, there were over 221 major demonstrations at over a hundred universities. The anti-war movement merged with other radical forms of protest – including civil rights, women's rights, and counterculture (see page 18).

The 1968 election

Johnson was so unpopular that he decided not to stand for re-election. His vice president, Hubert Humphrey, stood instead. Robert Kennedy, John Kennedy's brother, also ran on an anti-war platform. His assassination ensured Humphrey won the Democrat nomination. Nixon, standing on a slogan of 'Bringing the US Together', implied that he knew how to win the war, without saying how. There was also a third candidate – George Wallace, a southerner, who declared he would bomb North Vietnam back into the stone age. In the election Nixon won 43.4 per cent of the vote, Humphrey 42.7 per cent and Wallace 13.5 per cent, suggesting that the 'silent majority' still supported the war.

Nixon's presidency

Nixon steadily reduced the USA's commitment to South Vietnam. The 1970 US invasion of Cambodia briefly revived the anti-war movement. Four students were killed by National Guardsmen at Kent State University. By the 1972 presidential election, Nixon had reduced US troops in South Vietnam to 40,000. He won the election with 60 per cent of the vote. In 1973, he agreed to end all US combat activities in **Indo-China**.

The results of the war

In 1975, North Vietnamese forces overran South Vietnam and Vietnam was united. The Vietnam War, probably the most disastrous foreign policy adventure in the USA's history, had a damaging effect on the USA economically, socially and morally. It deeply divided Americans. Defeat also undermined American confidence.

Spectrum of importance

Below are a sample exam question and a list of general points, which could be used to answer the question. Use your own knowledge and the information on the opposite page to reach a judgement about the importance of these general points to the question posed. Write numbers on the spectrum below to indicate their relative importance. Having done this, write a brief justification of your placement, explaining why some of these factors are more important than others. The resulting diagram could form the basis of an essay plan.

How accurate is to say that the 'silent' majority of Americans supported the Vietnam War in the years 1963–73?

1 The influence of the Korean War

2 The start of the Vietnam War

3 The 1964 election

4 The escalation of the war, 1965–68

5 Student protest, 1967–68

6 The 1968 election

7 Nixon's de-escalation

8 The 1970 anti-war protests

9 The end of the war

←――→

Least important   Most important

Eliminate irrelevance

Below are a sample exam question and a paragraph written in answer to this question. Read the paragraph and identify parts of the paragraph that are not directly relevant to the question. Draw a line through the information that is irrelevant and justify your deletions in the margin.

How successful were mass protests in the USA in bringing an end to the Vietnam War?

Protests against the Vietnam War began in American universities in 1964. But at this stage President Johnson seemed to have most of the nation behind him with regard to Vietnam. Congress passed the Gulf of Tonkin Resolution, which authorised the president to take all necessary measures to repel any attack on US forces. Only two senators voted against the resolution, which Johnson thereafter interpreted as equivalent to a congressional declaration of war. Johnson also had a landslide victory over Barry Goldwater, the Republican candidate in the 1964 presidential election. But once US ground troops went into South Vietnam in 1965 and casualty rates went up, the protests escalated. During 1965 the number of US troops in Vietnam increased to around 200,000 and there were widespread protests. In April 1965 protesters marched on Washington. However, until 1968 it was mainly students who protested. But only a tenth of higher education institutions experienced serious anti-war disturbances and within those fewer than a tenth of students participated. Arguably the pre-1968 student protesters simply alienated the majority of Americans. The 1967 March on Washington, for example, had a hippy character that annoyed many older Americans. Had the USA been winning the war there might not have been protests. The USA's inability to win the war was the cause of the protests. The protests prior to 1968 certainly did not cause the USA's defeat or convince President Johnson to end the Vietnam War.

Exam focus

Below is sample high-level essay. Read it and the comments around it.

To what extent did Franklin Roosevelt prove himself a successful president on the domestic front in the years 1933–41?

Inaugurated in March 1933, Franklin Roosevelt remained president for the rest of his life. He had to deal with two great crises – the Depression and the Second World War. Virtually everything he did sparked intense controversy. He was both the most loved and the most hated president in the twentieth century. But the fact that he was re-elected in 1936, 1940 and 1944 suggests that most Americans had confidence in him. With good cause. This essay will argue that he had proved himself a very successful president on the domestic front by 1941 – just as he was to prove himself a great war leader post-1941.

From the start of his presidency, Roosevelt pervaded optimism and self-confidence. In his inaugural address, he proclaimed, 'The only thing we have to fear is fear itself'. He declared he would ask Congress for broad executive powers to wage war against the emergency. According to historian William Leuchtenburg, the address, which helped instill hope and courage, was Roosevelt's 'greatest single contribution to the politics of the 1930s'. Roosevelt chose a strong team to tackle the crisis. Cabinet members like Harold Ickes, secretary of the interior, played crucial roles. So did members of his 'Brain Trust' – advisers like Samuel Rosenman and Rexford Tugwell. Roosevelt was lucky that Congress was dominated by the Democrats and by the fact that the economic crisis meant that he was able to count on an extraordinary amount of co-operation. But he was the man who led and shaped the immediate recovery package – the Hundred Days.

One of Roosevelt's greatest strengths was the fact that he was receptive to new ideas. 'It is common sense to take a method and try it', he said. 'If it fails, admit it frankly and try another. But above all try something.' Another strength was his ability to 'sell' his ideas to both Congress and the public. He projected a sense of utter self-confidence and emanated optimism. Journalists liked him and the banter of his frequent press conferences was translated in newspapers into a president in command of his job. He had faults. He was loath to admit mistakes. He was a poor administrator. He often prevaricated. But he proved himself a masterly politician. His main function – by no means an easy one – was to reconcile the sharply conflicting views of his reform-minded supporters.

Roosevelt's main concern in 1933 was to get the USA on the road to recovery. He was also aware that the Depression provided an opportunity to effect major social reforms which would help 'have-nots' in the future. The extent of the success of his New Deal measures continues to divide historians. It is certainly possible to claim that the New Deal was not very successful. At best, it brought about only partial economic recovery. Not until 1941 would full employment and prosperity return, and only then because of the war and rearmament. Many of his work programmes were inefficient, doing little to enhance skills. Roosevelt's social reform measures were limited. Welfare payments were not generous. Many groups were excluded from pensions and from unemployment insurance. Right-wing critics claim that Roosevelt went too far in terms of government intervention. By setting up too many overlapping and inefficient agencies, he created something close to administrative anarchy. It may be that the agencies got in the way of recovery. Arguably, whatever success there was occurred despite New Deal policies, not because of them. Left-

This is a confident and well-informed introduction, very much linked to the set question. It paves the way for what is likely to follow.

This paragraph examines, quite succinctly, the situation in 1933. It shows detailed knowledge of dates, names and events. The two quotes are very effective. The last sentence links back to the question in that it claims Roosevelt was *the* man.

This paragraph examines Roosevelt's qualities. It does well to provide a balanced picture. Roosevelt did have faults as well as strengths. The last sentence is perceptive.

This is a meaty, important paragraph which examines Roosevelt's aims and the various criticisms of the New Deal. Given the statement in the introduction, the essay must now go on to defend Roosevelt.

wing critics claim that Roosevelt did not go far enough. They stress that many measures benefited privileged groups, not the weak. There was little redistribution of wealth and big business was left intact.

However, most historians stress the New Deal's achievements. Roosevelt had no wish to destroy capitalism: his aim was to save it. He succeeded – by skilfully regulating it. His measures brought jobs, electricity and hope to some of America's most depressed areas. They introduced much-needed controls on banks. They gave the USA new roads, dams, hospitals and public buildings. They laid the foundations of the American welfare state. While not eradicating poverty or economic inequalities, the New Deal did begin to deploy the federal government's resources on behalf of those who had received little help in the past. Although it is too much to claim that Roosevelt saved the USA from revolution, he did restore national morale. Roosevelt gave almost all Americans a stake in the country at a time when despair and alienation elsewhere led to dictatorship. This was no small achievement.

The New Deal was also a successful political slogan, helping Roosevelt win presidential elections in 1932, 1936 and 1940. By constructing a coalition that included the South, organised labour, the intelligentsia and the poor, Roosevelt ensured that the Democrats replaced the Republicans as the normal majority party. While Roosevelt's government may have done little to redistribute wealth, it did redistribute power between capital and labour. In legitimising and strengthening trade unions, Roosevelt helped them to secure generous wages and benefits for their members.

'Not bad. Not bad at all', was Reagan's summary of his presidency. Far more praise should be lavished on Roosevelt's performance between 1933–41. Not all his New Deal measures were successful. Not all were 'new'. From first to last, Roosevelt was reluctant to engage in massive deficit spending. He hankered after balancing the budget. Nevertheless, his measures did create jobs and hope. He also founded the modern American welfare state based on the concept that the federal government had a responsibility to guarantee a minimum standard of living. In expanding the authority of the federal government, Roosevelt had transformed the institution of the presidency, becoming in Leuchtenburg's view 'the first modern president'. The presidency became the centre stage of political life, the focus of Americans' hopes and expectations. Roosevelt gave Americans hope and expectations. The eight years from 1933 to 1941 were years of considerable success – success which paved the way for Roosevelt's greater success in 1941–45.

A concise paragraph with a clear analytical link to the question. The paragraph is full of relevant detail – without getting bogged down in the 'alphabet soup' of the New Deal. The short, understated last sentence is again effective. It's a good thing to end a paragraph on a high!

A short but important paragraph on Roosevelt's political success – which is often forgotten. The paragraph, like all the rest, displays a really good understanding of the situation and connects with the question.

The conclusion does what every good conclusion should do: it pulls together the argument that was initiated in the introduction and developed throughout the essay. It presents a balanced and thoroughly consistent argument. The first sentence of the conclusion is good. The last points to the fact that Roosevelt was even more successful as a war leader.

This is a Level 5 essay due to the fact that it engages with the question and has a clear, balanced and carefully reasoned argument that is sustained throughout. The essay is very well written, clearly structured and displays an impressive depth of knowledge. It uses valid criteria to substantiate an overall judgement.

Reverse engineering

The best essays are based on careful plans. Read the essay and the comments and try to work out the general points of the plan used to write the essay. Once you have done this, note down the specific examples used to support each general point.

2 The quest for civil rights, 1917–80

Life in the South and the impact of northern migration, 1917–32

The South, 1917–32

In 1917, over 80 per cent of black Americans lived in the South. Despite the **14th** and **15th Amendments** to the Constitution, Southern blacks remained economically, legally, socially and politically inferior.

Poverty, segregation and discrimination

- Most black people were impoverished **sharecroppers**.
- All aspects of southern life – schools, restaurants, hospitals, prisons, even graveyards – were segregated.
- Segregation, according to the *Plessy v Ferguson* **ruling** (1896), was supposedly meant to follow the rule 'separate but equal'. Yet black facilities were invariably inferior to white facilities.
- Southern whites used a variety of means to keep blacks from voting. Blacks had to pay an expensive poll tax, pass literacy tests or prove their grandfathers had voted.
- **'Uppity'** blacks: who challenged white authority, faced the threat of being lynched by white mobs.

Black success

Ironically, segregation meant that some black Americans were more prosperous than others. There were black doctors, lecturers, churchmen, shopkeepers and so on. Some black leaders did their best to improve conditions.

- Booker T. Washington, influential after 1895, regarded economic improvement and education as the first necessary step for blacks. Until this was achieved, he believed blacks should accept segregation.
- W.E.B. Du Bois aimed at legal and political equality for blacks. He established the National Association for the Advancement of Colored People (NAACP) in 1909. The NAACP tried to promote black equality and desegregation through the law courts.

Northern migration

After 1910, large numbers of blacks migrated to northern cities, for various reasons, but mainly because they:
- found better-paid jobs, particularly after 1914 when the First World War stimulated US manufacturing
- could vote
- were unlikely to be lynched.

Northern segregation and discrimination

Blacks in the North, however, were still essentially segregated. They congregated in the poorer parts of cities in what became known as '**ghettos**'. Discrimination, along with limited educational and employment opportunities, made it hard to get out of the ghetto. The onset of Depression in 1929 particularly hit northern blacks hard, with many losing their jobs.

Race riots

Working-class whites resented black competition for jobs and housing. Riots frequently resulted, especially in 1919 after soldiers returned from the First World War. The worst occurred in Chicago: 23 blacks and 15 whites were killed.

Black pride and white power

In the early 1920s, black pride and white power groups thrived.

Black pride

Marcus Garvey, born in Jamaica, founded the Universal Negro Improvement Association (UNIA) in 1914. He aimed to make blacks proud of themselves and their culture. Establishing himself in **Harlem**, Garvey was an inspiring speaker and edited *Negro World*, which soon had a circulation of over 100,000. But Garvey's support for separatism (setting the black race apart from the white race) antagonised Du Bois and NAACP. After Garvey was deported in 1927, the UNIA quickly collapsed.

The Ku Klux Klan (KKK)

The Klan had grown up in the South after the **Civil War**, aiming to maintain white supremacy. Prosecuted by the government, it had quickly declined. It was re-founded in 1915. Recruitment was assisted by the film *Birth of a Nation*, which glorified Klan members as defenders of white civilisation. The new Klan, which had far more members than the old, was national rather than simply southern. Many white northerners and westerners resented blacks and Catholic and Jewish immigrants from Europe. By 1925 the Klan had 5 million members and dominated legislatures in several states. A series of scandals, however, led to the movement's decline in the late 1920s.

Complete the paragraph

Below are a sample exam-style question and a paragraph written in answer to this question. The paragraph contains a point and specific examples, but lacks a concluding analytical link back to the question. Complete the paragraph by adding this link in the space provided.

To what extent did southern black Americans who migrated north exchange a disadvantaged rural life for a disadvantaged urban life in the years 1917–32?

By 1917, large numbers of southern black Americans had migrated to northern, midwestern and western cities such as Chicago, Detroit and New York. The industrialised cities offered more and better paid jobs, especially during the First World War when there was a shortage of workers. However, life was not necessarily easy for black Americans who lived in the North. The influx of black Americans into the cities caused deterioration in race relations in many areas. Northern cities began to pass residential segregation laws. Working-class white Americans resented black American competition for jobs and housing. Race riots frequently resulted, especially in 1919. In the northern and western cities, black Americans were usually forced to live in poor areas — or ghettos. Discrimination and limited educational and employment opportunities, especially after 1929, made it hard to get out of the ghetto. Thus,

_____

_____

_____

Identify key terms

Below is a sample exam question which includes a key word or term. Key terms are important because their meaning can be helpful in structuring your answer, developing an argument and establishing criteria that will help form the basis of a judgement.

How accurate is to say that black Americans suffered just as much discrimination in the North and West as in the South in the years 1917–32?

- First, identify the key word or term. This will be a word or phrase that is important to the meaning of the question. Underline the word or phrase.
- Secondly, define the key phrase. Your definition should set out the key features of the phrase or word that you are defining.
- Third, make an essay plan that reflects your definition.
- Finally, write a sentence answering the question that refers back to the definition.

Now repeat the task, and consider how the change in key terms affects the structure, argument and final judgement of your essay.

To what extent did black Americans face problems of segregation in the South and in northern and western cities in the years 1917–32?

The impact of the New Deal, the Second World War and Truman's presidency

The impact of the New Deal

It is difficult to be sure of Roosevelt's aims with regard to blacks.

Do nothing?

Given Roosevelt's dependence upon southern Democrat support in Congress, it would have been political suicide to have gone out of his way to help black Americans. Accordingly, he did not support a number of anti-lynching bills.

Do something?

- As a disproportionate number of the poor were black, Roosevelt's New Deal programmes affected them greatly. One million black Americans obtained jobs through the New Deal.
- Roosevelt made a significant number of appointments promoting black Americans to senior positions in the federal bureaucracy.
- Roosevelt's wife, Eleanor, spoke in favour of civil rights.
- Black Americans believed Roosevelt had their interests at heart. Before 1932, those who could vote usually voted Republican (Abraham Lincoln's party). By 1936, they overwhelmingly voted Democrat.

The effect of the Second World War

The war generally had a positive impact on the civil rights movement.

Positive impact

- During the war, two million blacks moved from the South to northern and western cities, mainly to find better jobs.
- In 1941, Roosevelt issued Executive Order 8802. Its aim was to end discrimination because of race, creed, colour or national origin in the defence industries and the government.
- Many black Americans trained for military leadership. Black officers commanded black regiments.
- Many black servicemen were based in Britain, where they experienced life with less prejudice.
- The US fight against Nazi Germany inspired more black Americans to campaign against their own lack of freedom and equality. Black leaders pointed out that the evils of Nazism were in many ways replicated in the racist South. Many white Americans recognised the justice of this claim.

- A new and more militant organisation, the Congress of Racial Equality (CORE), was established in 1942 (see page 32).
- NAACP membership rose from 50,000 in 1940 to 450,000 by 1945.
- In 1945–46, many black veterans took advantage of the GI Bill to go to college or learn a skilled trade. These educated professionals and technicians helped expand the black middle class that was important in the 1950s and 60s civil rights movement.

Negative impact

- American forces remained segregated during the war.
- Many trade unions continued to exclude black Americans, who were mainly assigned low-level jobs.
- Many white workers resented black workers. In 1943 there were some 250 'hate strikes' and race riots in US cities.

Truman's presidency

Truman, openly racist in his youth, developed a sense of responsibility towards black Americans. He was determined to stand up to Communism and realised that racial discrimination had the potential to discredit the USA. America claimed to stand for freedom, democracy and equality. Segregation was the weak point in its moral armoury. Truman thus aimed to eliminate the greatest abuses from American life.

Truman's actions

- A Committee on Civil Rights, set up in 1946, produced a report entitled *To Secure These Rights*. This called for an end to segregation. The Committee's revolutionary recommendations were ignored by Congress.
- In 1948, Truman issued an executive order aimed at ending segregation in the US armed forces by 1954. This process was speeded up by the Korean War.
- Truman used his executive powers to give equal employment opportunities in the federal bureaucracy.
- He appointed black Americans to significant posts.
- He used federal purchasing power to try to coax businessmen into equal employment practices.

It could be that Truman's actions were limited in extent and were largely aimed at winning the black northern vote. Nevertheless, he increased public awareness of the need for change.

You're the examiner

Below are a sample exam question and a paragraph written in answer to this question. Read the paragraph and the mark scheme provided on pages 109–10. Decide which level you would award the paragraph. Write the level below, along with a justification for your choice.

To what extent were black civil rights enhanced in the years 1933–53?

> The New Deal did much to alleviate black poverty. One million black Americans obtained jobs through the New Deal. Eleanor Roosevelt achieved small but concrete victories that also helped to raise black morale. Roosevelt himself also used the traditional method of making significant appointments. By the late 1930s there were nearly 50 black Americans in senior positions. In some respects, this was very limited reform. Roosevelt's dependence upon southern Democrats in Congress meant he dare not articulate any great desire to help black Americans. He did not fully support anti-lynching bills in 1934, 1935 and 1938. However, most black Americans felt that Roosevelt had their interests at heart. Traditionally, blacks had voted for the Republican Party, the party of Abraham Lincoln. By 1936 most blacks who voted, voted Democrat — and continued to do so. By giving black Americans both jobs and hope, Roosevelt had enhanced the black civil rights cause at the most basic — but perhaps most important — level.

Level:

Mark:

Reason for choosing this level and this mark:

_____

_____

Turning assertion into argument

Below are a sample exam-style question and a series of assertions. Read the exam question and then add a justification to each of the assertions to turn it into an argument.

How far do you agree that the aims and policies of Roosevelt and Truman greatly assisted black Americans in the years 1933–53?

> Roosevelt's New Deal programmes, while not specifically designed to help black Americans, aided black Americans in the sense that...

> Although the USA's armed forces remained segregated in the Second World War, the war helped black Americans in the sense that...

> Both the Second World War and Cold War, fought against perceived 'evil' regimes, helped the civil rights movement in the sense that...

> Although Truman's main aim was to win the growing northern black vote, his policies helped the civil rights movement in the sense that...

From legal challenge to direct action, 1917–55

Legal challenge

The NAACP, established in 1909 by Du Bois, tried to promote black equality through the law courts. Initially, the NAACP did not attract much support or achieve much success in the South. In 1934, disagreements resulted in Du Bois leaving the organisation. He was succeeded by Walter White.

The NAACP's actions, 1934–55

White used a variety of methods to promote civil rights through the NAACP:
- He worked with trade unionists, churches and white liberals to forge a coalition to persuade the **House of Representatives** to promote anti-lynching bills.
- The NAACP mobilised southern blacks to campaign for the abolition of the poll tax.
- Continuing its work through the law courts, the NAACP used black lawyers such as Thurgood Marshall.

NAACP's achievements

NAACP's legal campaigns achieved several triumphs:
- The Supreme Court's decision in *Smith v Allwright* (1944) made it easier for black Americans to vote in the South.
- In 1950, the Supreme Court ruled that a black student could attend a white Texan law school that was superior to the local black one.
- In *Brown v Board of Education, Topeka* (1954), the Supreme Court ruled that schools should be desegregated, reversing the *Plessy v Ferguson* decision (1896) (see page 28). This was a landmark ruling – the starting point for the civil rights movements of the mid-twentieth century. However, the ruling set no timetable for action, and merely asked for 'all due speed'.

The NAACP increased black awareness. Its range of methods set an important example for the civil rights organisations that developed post-1955.

Direct action

Although black Americans became more assertive, black leaders rejected violence as a solution to racial problems.

James Farmer and CORE

James Farmer aimed to achieve black equality in an integrated society. In 1942, he established the Congress of Racial Equality (CORE). CORE's methods were more militant than those of the NAACP. During the 1940s it organised:
- **sit-ins** at segregated Chicago restaurants
- 'Freedom Rides' in North/South border states to try to ensure the enforcement of Supreme Court rulings on desegregation in interstate transport.

CORE's achievements were limited by 1955 but its methods paved the way for future civil rights activism.

The Montgomery bus boycott

In 1955, NAACP activist **Rosa Parks** challenged the bus segregation policy of Montgomery, Alabama. Deliberately sitting in a 'white' seat, she was arrested and tried. Her arrest electrified the local black community. NAACP enlisted black church leaders to organise, inspire and finance a bus boycott in protest. Boycotts were not new: black Americans had used them with varying degrees of success since 1900. But this boycott had a major impact mainly because of:
- media attention – particularly television
- the leadership of Reverend **Martin Luther King Jr.**

The boycott, which lasted over a year and nearly bankrupted the city's bus companies, brought an end to segregation on Montgomery's buses in December 1956.

The situation in 1955

Propaganda, pressure-group agitation and economic and political factors had begun to have an effect on segregation:
- Many universities and colleges were desegregated.
- The major leagues in baseball, basketball and American football were desegregated.
- More southern black Americans could vote.
- By 1955, more black Americans were being elected and appointed to office in the Upper South.
- Black Americans were beginning to make an important contribution to literature and particularly to music, as blues and rock and roll began to influence young white Americans.

While segregation was in retreat across much of America, many white Americans in the **Deep South** were determined to maintain white supremacy.

Simple essay style

Below is a sample exam question. Use your own knowledge and the information on the opposite page to produce a plan for this question. Choose four general points, and provide three pieces of specific information to support each general point. Once you have planned your essay, write the introduction and conclusion for the essay. The introduction should list the points to be discussed in the essay. The conclusion should summarise the key points and justify which point was the most important.

How successful was the NAACP in the years 1917–55?

Complete the paragraph

Below are a sample exam-style question and a paragraph written in answer to this question. The paragraph contains a point and specific examples, but lacks a concluding analytical link back to the question. Complete the paragraph by adding this link in the space provided.

How accurate is it to say that legal challenge was more successful than direct action in the fight for civil rights in the years 1917–55?

The NAACP achieved a great deal in the period 1917–45. Walter White's legal campaign achieved several triumphs. Thurgood Marshall worked hard to pressurise the Supreme Court into ruling that that unequal expenditure on black and white higher education was against the 14th Amendment. Another Supreme Court decision (*Smith v Allwright*, 1944) made it easier for blacks to vote in the South. The NAACP was also developing into an effective pressure group, demonstrating that it was possible for a black organisation to influence Congress. It succeeded in increasing black awareness. Its effectiveness in galvanising black Americans into fighting for their rights can be seen in the rise of its membership — from 50,000 in 1940 to 450,000 in 1945. Overall,

_____

_____

_____

Changing patterns and approaches, 1955–68

Eisenhower's presidency

While doubting the wisdom of the *Brown v Board of Education, Topeka* ruling that schools be desegregated, Eisenhower accepted the necessity of upholding federal law.

Little Rock, Arkansas

In 1957, nine black students tried to attend Central High School in Little Rock, Arkansas. When white students, supported by State Governor Faubus, tried to stop them entering, Eisenhower sent federal troops to Little Rock and federalised Arkansas's **National Guard** so it was under his command, not that of Faubus.

Civil Rights Acts

Civil Rights Acts were passed in 1957 and 1960. While not going far, they were the first such measures to pass since the late-nineteenth century.

Martin Luther King

Martin Luther King Jr established the Southern Christian Leadership Conference (SCLS) in 1957. He aimed to end segregation and to gain political equality for Southern blacks. Influenced by **Gandhi**'s tactics in India, he determined to use non-violent means of protest.

Sit-ins

In 1960, students in Greensboro, North Carolina, successfully used Farmer's 'sit-in' method at an all-white Woolworth's cafe. This action was copied across the South in segregated cafes, hotels and libraries. Boycotts supplemented sit-ins, pray-ins and stand-ins. No one organisation co-ordinated the action. A variety of organisations were involved:
- the Congress of Racial Equality (CORE)
- the Southern Christian Leadership Conference (SCLC)
- and the Student Non-violent Co-ordinating Committee (SNCC).

Ministers of black churches played an important role. Sometimes segregation ended quietly, and sometimes white Americans responded with violence.

Kennedy's presidency

JFK's commitment to civil rights was far from total. He tended, initially, to be reactive rather than proactive.

Grassroots activity

Non-violent action continued in the South.

- In 1961, Freedom Riders challenged interstate transport segregation.

- King used peaceful marches to draw attention to segregation and **disfranchisement**.
- In 1962, James Meredith challenged segregation in the University of Mississippi.
- The SCLL, SNCC and NAACP worked together on voter registration in Mississippi.
- In 1963, there were over a thousand desegregation protests across the South.

King's importance

King was generally recognised as the leader of the civil rights movement, although in many ways the movement made him rather than he made the movement. King performed well on television and was an excellent orator – as proved by his 'I have a dream' speech at the climax of a 250,000-strong march on Washington in 1963. Frequently arrested for leading marches, he was aware that this drew national attention to injustice. Sometimes he deliberately provoked a violent white reaction in order to publicise his cause, as in Birmingham, Alabama, in 1963.

Kennedy's commitment

By 1962, Kennedy was committed to civil rights.

- He supported his brother Robert Kennedy, the **attorney general**, who worked to desegregate transportation and other facilities.
- He sent troops to Mississippi to support James Meredith and also to Birmingham, Alabama.
- In 1963, he supported a wide-ranging Civil Rights Bill, which got bogged down in Congress.

Johnson's presidency

Johnson had long been committed to civil rights.

Civil Rights Act

In 1964, LBJ pushed Kennedy's bill through Congress. It:
- set up an Equal Employment Commission
- ensured desegregation of schools
- outlawed segregation in public facilities
- strengthened black American voting rights.

Other actions

- In 1965, a Voting Act eliminated restrictive practices designed to keep blacks from voting.
- A 1968 Civil Rights Act banned discrimination in housing.
- Johnson's War on Poverty (see page 76) assisted blacks, the USA's poorest group.

Johnson thus made a greater contribution to civil rights than any other president.

! Complete the paragraph

a

Below are a sample exam-style question and a paragraph written in answer to this question The paragraph contains a point and a concluding explanatory link back to the question, but lacks examples. Complete the paragraph by adding examples in the space provided.

How accurate is it to say Martin Luther King made the civil rights movement in the years 1957–68?

> The role of King within the civil rights movement was of huge significance in the year 1963. For example,
>
> _____
>
> _____
>
> _____
>
> Accordingly, King was undoubtedly one of the main leaders of the civil rights movement in 1963. However, this does not mean that he made the movement. Arguably the reverse was true: the movement made him.

⚡ RAG – rate the timeline

Below are a sample exam question and a timeline. Read the question, study the timeline and, using three coloured pens, put a red, amber or green star next to the events to show:

Red: events and policies that have no relevance to the question

Amber: events and policies that have some significance to the question

Green: events and policies that are directly relevant to the question.

1 To what extent did Martin Luther King lead the civil rights movement in the years 1957–68?

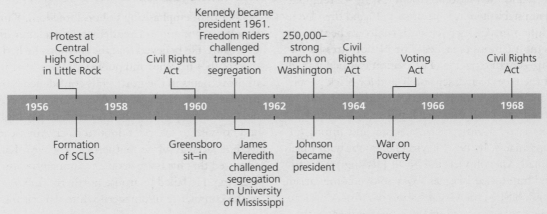

Now repeat the activity with the following questions:

2 How far did American presidents assist the civil rights movement in the years 1957–68?

3 To what extent had civil rights been successful in the years 1957–68?

The emergence of Black Power and King's northern strategy

Northern riots

In 1964, northern and western cities experienced riots in the ghettos. The riots continued for the next four years. In 1965, in the Watts district of Los Angeles, there were six days of rioting. Thirty-four people were killed and 900 injured. In 1967, there were 43 deaths in Detroit. The riots were perceived to arise from black poverty in the North, where there was **de facto segregation** in housing and schools. In 1967–68, a National Advisory Committee on Civil Disorder, headed by Governor Kerner, warned of the danger of the USA splitting into two warring civilisations – black and white. He also stated the need for a massive federal aid programme for the ghettos. However, northern black American demands for equal economic opportunity proved far more challenging than southern civil rights.

Black Power

Some northern blacks supported 'Black Power'.

Malcolm X

Malcolm X was the most important voice of Black Power. As a young man he was sentenced to a 10-year jail sentence for drugs, pimping and armed robbery. In prison he converted to the Nation of Islam (NOI) – a religious movement established in Detroit in 1930 and then led by Elijah Muhammad. Once released, Malcolm became the Nation's most famous preacher. The Nation stressed the evil nature of white people. The Nation claimed it made sense for the races to live separately and for black people to develop an independent American nation. Thanks to Malcolm efforts, NOI membership rose to 40,000. His opponents accused him of 'black racism' and aiming for 'black supremacy'. In 1964, having fallen out with Elijah Muhammad, Malcolm left the NOI. His pilgrimage to Mecca led him to see Islam as a way to overcome racism. He then established the Organisation of Afro-American Unity. He was assassinated in 1965, by members of the Nation of Islam.

Other Black Power individuals/movements

- Separatists (see page 28) infiltrated and took over some of the main civil rights organisations, for example, CORE and the SNCC.

- Stokely Carmichael popularised the slogans 'Black Power', 'Black is beautiful' and 'Back to Africa'. 'If we don't get justice we're going to tear this country apart', he declared.

- In 1966, ex-criminals Huey Newton and Bobby Seale founded the Black Panther Party in California. Willing to ally with white radicals, their symbols were the shoot-out and the gun. Members engaged in petty crime and sought confrontation with police officers. However, their 30 urban **chapters** won considerable respect in the ghettos, especially for their emphasis on self-help. They established clinics to advise on health, welfare and legal rights. They also provided childcare for working mothers and set up a Free Breakfast programme.

Most Black Power groups had few members. (The Black Panthers never boasted more than 5,000 members.) They were also divided. Police easily infiltrated their ranks. Many of their leaders were killed or imprisoned.

King's northern strategy

After 1965, King turned his attention to the northern ghettos.

Economic justice

Rather than emphasising political freedom, King began to stress economic justice, demanding a fairer distribution of wealth. He believed that the methods he had used in the South – marches and publicity – would achieve improvements in the north. His confidence proved misplaced. Northern white Americans opposed his northern strategy. Most had no wish to pay higher taxes and no wish to live next door to black Americans. Many were as racist as white southerners. By 1967, King admitted that his Poor People's Campaign wasn't working. He failed to arouse northern black Americans or the conscience of northern white Americans.

King's assassination

In April 1968, King was assassinated by a white man in Memphis. As many as 125 ghettos erupted in rage, and 70,000 troops were needed to end the riots. Forty-six people died, 2,000 were injured, 21,000 were arrested and property valued at $67 million was damaged.

Mind map

Use the information on the opposite page to add detail (at least two points) to the mind map below.

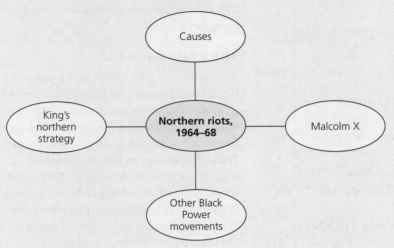

Causes

King's northern strategy — **Northern riots, 1964–68** — Malcolm X

Other Black Power movements

Develop the detail

a

Below are a sample exam-style question and a paragraph written in answer to this question. The paragraph contains a limited amount of detail. Annotate the paragraph to add additional detail to the answer.

How successful was the Black Power movement in the years 1964–68?

Malcolm X was one of the main leaders of the Black Power movement. He appealed to poor Northern blacks. But he attracted far more opponents than supporters. In 1964, he split with the Nation of Islam. He was assassinated in 1965.

The impact of civil rights legislation, 1955–80

The success of the civil rights movement

In many ways, it seems evident that the civil rights movement had been successful.

Achievements

- Segregation and the most overt forms of discrimination came to an end.
- Most white supremacists/racists were removed from office.
- Blacks had increased their political power. There were an increased number of elected and appointed black officials.
- In the late 1960s and 70s there were a number of 'affirmative action programmes' to help blacks gain places in universities and jobs.
- Bussing was introduced to try and end segregation in schools.
- By 1980, more than a third of American blacks were categorised as middle class.
- The civil rights movement encouraged other minorities – Native Americans, Hispanic Americans and gays – to claim the birthright of equality.

Reasons for success

- General worldwide ideology was important. The Third World was on the rise as European empires collapsed. The USA, anxious to attract support in the Cold War, could not be seen to deny freedom and equality to a seventh of its own people.
- US presidents, especially Johnson, deserve credit.
- Supreme Court verdicts in favour of civil rights were crucial.
- Television played a role in convincing white opinion that the situation in the South had to change.
- A number of black grassroot movements played a crucial role, especially NAACP, CORE, SNCC and SCLC.
- There were a similar number of grassroot black heroes and heroines, perhaps the most important of whom was King.

Limits of success

The civil rights movement was far from totally successful, however.

The white backlash

Northern riots after 1964 and the perceived threat of Black Power meant that blacks lost a lot of white sympathy. Most northern whites disliked affirmative action programmes and bussing. In the South, white supremacists did not disappear. Many voted for George Wallace when he ran for the presidency in 1968. Wallace might have done even better in 1972 but was shot by a would-be assassin and left paralysed below the waist. Blacks received relatively little support from presidents Nixon, Ford and Carter. Nixon's aim was to win southern whites for the Republican Party. He got barely 5 per cent of the black vote in 1968 and 1972. He opposed bussing and cut back on Johnson's Poverty programmes. Carter, the ex-governor of Georgia, won the black vote in 1976 but thereafter did little for blacks.

Black problems, 1969–80

The riots that beset the USA in the 1960s died down in the 1970s. However, the black ghettos had not gone away. In both the North and South blacks remained the poorest group. The USA suffered considerable economic problems in the 1970s, including a rise in unemployment. Blacks were more likely to be unemployed in the 1970s – as they had been in the 1930s. De facto segregation continued to exist in housing and education. A great deal of crime was committed by blacks; it was also done to blacks by other blacks. Much of the crime was drug-related. The majority of black children grew up in single-parent families. It seemed to many that the USA still had a black underclass by 1980 – just as it had in 1920, 1940 and 1960.

Developing an argument

Below is a sample exam-style question, a list of key points to be made in the essay and a paragraph from the essay. Read the question, the plan and the sample paragraph. Rewrite the paragraph in order to develop an argument. Your paragraph should explain why the factor discussed in the paragraph is linked to the question. Crucially, it should develop an argument by setting out a general answer to the question and reasons that support this.

How successful was the civil rights movement in the years 1955–80?

Key points

- The situation in 1955.
- Black grassroots action, 1955–68.
- Presidential and Congressional action.
- The situation by 1980.

In 1955, Southern blacks usually lived in all-black, run-down neighbourhoods. Black children attended all-black and mostly inferior schools. Most reputable higher and further education colleges and universities were closed to blacks. Blacks could not go to cinemas, hotels, restaurants, swimming pools and parks frequented by whites. Many employers rejected black applicants on grounds of colour, so most blacks found themselves confined to occupations considered 'menial' by whites. Southern blacks, for the most part, were not allowed to vote, and were routinely harassed by white law enforcement officials. In the North, blacks were not much better off. They lived in poor housing and attended poor schools. Although they could vote, they were economically and socially disadvantaged.

Recommended reading

Below is a list of suggested further reading on this section.

- *Years of Discord: American Politics and Society, 1961–1974*, pages 67–75, 102–12, 117–24, 164–70, 252–70, John Morton Blum (1991)
- *Grand Expectations, The United States, 1945–74*, pages 19–31, 374–406, 468–85, 579–88, 652–68, James T. Patterson (1996)
- *An Introduction to American History 1860–1990*, pages 157–99, Alan Farmer and Vivienne Sanders (2002)

Native Americans and Hispanic American civil right campaigns, 1960–80

Native American rights

Native Americans (previously called Indians) emerged as a new political force in the late 1960s.

Native American problems

In 1960, the Native Americans' plight was more desperate than any other minority group.

- Many lived on reservations.
- Unemployment was ten times the national rate.
- Life expectancy was 20 years lower than the national average.
- The suicide rate was a hundred times higher than the rate for whites.
- Alcoholism was a widespread problem.

If blacks had managed to extract a promise of compensation for past injustices, Native Americans felt they had an even more compelling claim on white consciences. Many whites agreed. The Eisenhower administration tried to promote Native American assimilation and end tribal **sovereignty**, while Johnson's War on Poverty channelled increased federal funds to reservations.

Native American actions

Between 1968 and 1975, Native American activists forced American society to hear their demands.

- In 1968, the American Indian Movement (AIM) was founded on the promise of advancing 'Red Power'.
- In 1969, AIM leaders occupied Alcatraz Island in San Francisco Bay. The protest lasted 19 months and involved more than 400 people from 50 different tribes, helping to consolidate a unified Native American approach to activism.
- In 1972 a sit-in at the Bureau of Indian Affairs in Washington attracted national attention.

More moderate activists, working through organisations such as the National Congress of American Indians, lobbied Congress for greater rights and resources.

Native American protesters soon discovered a more effective tactic than direct action. They went into federal courts armed with copies of old treaties and demanded that past legal injustices should be righted. In Alaska, Maine and Massachusetts they won significant settlements that provided legal recognition of their tribal rights and considerable financial compensation.

Hispanic Americans

In the 1960s, Hispanics campaigned for political and economic action.

Hispanic growth

Thanks to immigration and a high birth rate, the Hispanic population soared. In 1960, Hispanics numbered 3 million. By 1980, they numbered 20 million. The most numerous were Mexican Americans, concentrated in California and the Southwest. Next came the Puerto Ricans, most of whom lived in New York. Finally, there were Cubans, mainly refugees from **Fidel Castro**'s regime, concentrated in southern Florida.

Hispanic problems

Most Hispanics were poor. They were also isolated from mainstream American life by the language barrier. The belief that Hispanics were entitled to schooling in Spanish as well as English divided the Hispanic community. Some wished to promote their heritage. Others feared that failure to adopt English as their main language would block their advance.

Mexican Americans

In 1970, there were some 9 million Mexican Americans. Most endured many of the same disabilities as blacks – high unemployment, poor housing, educational segregation and discriminatory treatment by the police. By the 1970s, some 85 per cent of Mexican Americans lived in cities (especially Los Angeles), inhabiting their own generally run-down areas – or barrios. In rural areas, poverty was widespread.

Economic action

The plight of Mexican American migrant farm workers was especially dire. In the 1960s, Cesar Chavez founded the United Farm Workers (UFW) in California. He then launched a series of strikes for an increase in the wages and benefits of migrant workers. By 1970, the UFW had won recognition from grape growers and national visibility for the plight of Hispanic farm labourers through well-publicised boycotts of grapes and lettuce. It won its fight for better wages and working conditions.

Chicanos' rights

In the late 1960s, young activists supported 'Brown Power'. Rather than seeking equal rights through integration, they sought to promote Mexican culture and ethnic heritage. Rejecting the term 'Mexican American' as demeaning, they called themselves Chicanos – a term drawn from barrio slang and associated with rebellious and sometimes criminal young men. Throughout the 1970s activists created a strong and unifying sense of cultural identity for Mexican American youth.

Simple essay style

Below is a sample exam question. Use your own knowledge and the information on the opposite page to produce a plan for this question. Choose four general points, and provide three pieces of specific information to support each general point. Once you have planned your essay, write the introduction and conclusion for the essay. The introduction should list the points to be discussed in the essay. The conclusion should summarise the key points and justify which point was the most important.

To what extent did Native Americans achieve success in their struggle for minority rights in the years 1960–80?

 Mind map

Use the information on the opposite page to add detail (at least two points) to the mind map below.

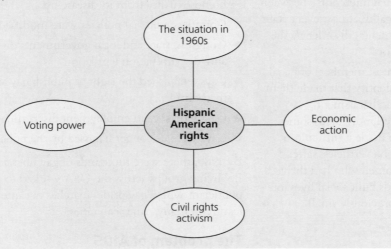

The emergence of the gay rights movement

Gay rights

The movement to protect gay and lesbian rights emerged after 1945.

The situation in 1950

The gay and lesbian civil rights movement was the product of repression and expansion.

- From the mid-1930s, homosexuality and cross-dressing had been increasingly penalised by US authorities. Gay people were treated as social outcasts. Homosexuality was grounds for dismissal from a job, expulsion from university and could even result in imprisonment. Consensual sexual intercourse between people of the same sex was illegal in almost every state. Homosexuality was labelled a mental disorder by the American Psychiatric Association.

- Gay men and lesbians, unlike most members of racial minorities, could conceal the identity that made them vulnerable to discrimination and harassment. Remaining 'in the closet' offered individuals some protection. But this option also made it difficult to organise a political movement. Nevertheless, after 1945, thousands of men and women who had thrived in the military's same-sex worlds built social lives for themselves that expanded the previously small homosexual subcultures.

The Mattachine Society

In 1950, several gay men founded the Mattachine Society in Los Angeles. They created a network of discussion groups where (mainly middle-class) men and women shared their experiences. Mattachine membership peaked in the thousands, with groups meeting across California and in New York and Chicago. In the 1960s, gay groups became more visible, staging small pickets in front of the White House to protest against the dismissal of gay federal employees.

Gay activism

On 27–28 June 1969 at New York's Stonewall Inn bar, gay patrons refused to disperse after a police raid. Street rioting ensued. As word spread, hundreds of New York gays joined the confrontation with the police which continued for several days. The Stonewall riot became a symbol of a new militancy. Joining groups like the Gay Activists Alliance and the Gay Liberation Front, activists campaigned for gay rights. Their main goals were to:

- decriminalise homosexual acts
- ensure equal treatment under the law
- ensure the dissemination of unbiased information about homosexuality

- encourage gays to come 'out of the closet' by announcing their homosexuality to friends, family and colleagues.

By 1973, some 800 gay organisations existed in the USA. They were concentrated in towns and cities and on university campuses.

Inspired by the civil rights movement, gays interrupted city council meetings and psychiatric conferences, had sit-ins at magazine offices and political campaign headquarters and marched through the streets. The militant tactics had some success.

- The American Psychiatric Association removed homosexuality from its disease list.
- Countless editorial policies were modified.
- Congress, state and local governments discussed anti-discrimination legislation.
- Gays established the right to publish gay and lesbian magazines.
- Gays won several employment discrimination cases.
- Gays were no longer harassed by the police.

By 1980, there were thousands of gay liberation groups. Lobbying groups across the USA worked to elect gay politicians while 'gay pride' marches became a common feature in many American cities.

The problem of AIDS

After 1980, the gay rights' movement increasingly turned its attention to combating acquired immunodeficiency syndrome (better known as AIDS). AIDS was caused by the human immunodeficiency virus (HIV) which attacked cells in the immune system. It spread through the exchange of blood or body fluids, often through sexual intercourse, leaving its victims susceptible to deadly infections and cancers. AIDS, which first emerged in the USA in 1981, quickly became epidemic among homosexual men. Politicians were slow to devote resources to combating AIDS, in part because it was initially perceived as a 'gay man's disease' which did not threaten other Americans. The gay movement mobilised to promote 'safe sex', prevent discrimination against people suffering from AIDS and press the federal government to devote greater resources to fighting the disease.

ⓘ Establish criteria

Below is a sample exam-style question which requires you to make a judgement. The key term in the question has been underlined. Defining the meaning of the key term can help you establish criteria that you can use to make a judgement.

Read the question, define the key term and then set out two or three criteria based on the key term, which you can use to reach and justify a judgement.

How accurate is it to say that <u>discrimination</u> against gay people was significantly reduced in the years 1950–80?

Definition:

_____

_____

Criteria to judge the extent to which discrimination against gay people was significantly reduced:

_____

_____

_____

_____

ⓘ Reach a judgement

Having defined the key term and established a series of criteria, you should now make a judgement. Consider how far discrimination against gay people had been reduced according to each criterion. Summarise your judgements below:

Criterion 1:

_____

Criterion 2:

_____

Criterion 3:

_____

Criterion 4:

_____

Finally, sum up your judgement. Based on the criteria, how accurate is it to say that discrimination against gay people was significantly reduced in the years 1950–80?

_____

_____

_____

_____

The achievements and limitations of the minority campaigns

Minority success?

In the more liberal atmosphere of the 1960s and 70s, and in the wake of the civil rights movement, various minority groups sought to end what they perceived (rightly in most cases) to be discrimination. Most had considerable success. Chicanos, Native Americans and gays all advanced their causes. But problems remained.

- Minority campaigns produced a backlash. The singling out of blacks, Chicanos and Native Americans for various kinds of federal aid produced a resentful reaction from other ethnic groups. Americans of Polish, Slovak, Italian and Greek origin protested that blacks and others officially classified as minorities were advancing at their expense. Thus in the late 1960s white ethnic community organisations echoed Black Power demands for neighbourhood improvement schemes, greater political representation and cultural recognition. This 'new ethnicity' was unsuccessful, largely because most descendants of southern and eastern Europeans were opposed to the idea of cultural distinctiveness.
- The white 'silent' majority, disapproved of much of what was happening, particularly with regard to affirmative action programmes. The result was a swing to the right politically, as reflected in Nixon's and Reagan's successes.
- The hope of speedy economic advancement did not come to pass for most minority groups.

Native American rights

Achievements

- Congress and the federal courts returned millions of acres of land to tribal ownership.
- In 1975, Congress passed the Indian Self-Determination and Education Assistance Act. This gave Native American leaders more control over education and economic development on the reservations.

Limitations

Conditions for most Native Americans remained grim during the 1970s and 1980s.

- Native Americans continued to have a higher rate of tuberculosis, alcoholism and suicide than any other group.
- Nine out of ten Native Americans lived in substandard housing.
- Unemployment rates for Native Americans were almost 40 per cent.

Hispanic American rights

Achievements

- The chief strength of the Hispanic movements lay less in copying civil rights strategies than in their numbers. Voter-registration drives resulted in the election of Chicanos to governorships in New Mexico and Arizona in 1974.
- By 1980, presidential candidates were courting the Hispanic vote, promising support for urban renewal projects in New York and amnesty programmes for illegal immigrants in Texas, and delivering anti-Castro speeches in Florida.
- A campaign for educational reform secured a speed up of school desegregation, the development of bilingual and bi-cultural courses and an increase in Chicano teachers.

Limitations

- The Chicano movement was not as influential nationally as the black civil rights movement.
- Hispanics continued to suffer discrimination in employment, housing, schools and in the courts.

Gay rights

Achievements

- By 1980, overt discrimination of gays had generally ended. The growth of public tolerance of homosexuality was among the most striking changes in American social attitudes in the last three decades of the twentieth century.
- By the 1980s, gays played an increasingly visible role in the social and political life of the USA.

Limitations

- Not all Americans liked or accepted the aims of the gay rights' movement.
- The Christian Coalition, founded by evangelical minister Pat Robertson, launched crusades against gay rights.
- Although many states and private corporations extended domestic-partner benefits to gay couples, the federal Defence of Marriage Act (1996) defined marriage as 'only' a union between one man and one woman.

Support or challenge?

Below is a sample exam-style question which asks you to what extent you agree with a specific statement. Below that is a list of general statements which are relevant to the question. Using your own knowledge and the information on the opposite page, decide whether these statements support or challenge the statement in question.

How accurate is it to say that the movements for Native Americans, Mexican Americans and gay rights achieved most of their aims in the years 1960–80?

STATEMENT	SUPPORT	CHALLENGE
The Indian Self-Determination and Education Assistance Act (1975) helped Native Americans.		
Native Americans continued to have higher rates of alcoholism and suicide than white Americans.		
By 1980, there were more Mexican American teachers.		
By 1980, Mexican Americans were elected to political office in increasing numbers.		
The Defence of Marriage Act (1996) was a success for homosexuals.		
By 1980, many gay people were willing to 'come out of the closet'.		

Introducing an argument

Below are an exam question, an essay plan and a basic introduction and conclusion. Rewrite the introduction and conclusion so that they contain an argument about how successful the minority movements were in achieving their aims in the years 1960–80.

How successful were the movements for Native American, Mexican American and gay rights in the years 1945–80?

Key points

- Native American rights: aims, achievements and limitations.
- Mexican American rights: aims, achievements and limitations.
- Gay rights: aims, achievements and limitations.

Introduction

In the years 1960–80, Native Americans, Mexican Americans (Chicanos) and gay people all sought to advance their causes, in particular to end discrimination. They did so in the wake of the civil rights movement. All three of the minority groups were generally successful in realising their aims.

Conclusion

In conclusion, Native Americans, Chicanos and gay people achieved most of their aims. However, there were still some problems to overcome.

Exam focus

Below is a sample high-level answer. Read it and the comments around it.

To what extent was Martin Luther King the leader of the civil rights movement in the years 1955–65?

Martin Luther King is generally assumed to be the leader of the civil rights movement in the crucial years 1955–65. There is good cause for this assumption. King was one of the leaders of the Montgomery, Alabama, bus boycott in 1955 and he led the demonstration in Selma, Alabama, which led to the Voting Rights Act in 1965. Along the way, he was the main civil rights spokesperson on television and was involved in most of the major civil rights protest movements of the period. However, as this essay will show, King was just one – albeit the most prominent – of many civil rights leaders. No single person led the movement. No single person made the movement. The movement certainly made King rather than he the movement. This is not to deny King his place in history. For without King, the civil rights movement would probably not have achieved the success it did.

> This introduction is well focused. It deals confidently with many of the crucial events and issues and gives a very clear indication of the likely course of the essay.

King first came to the fore in the Montgomery bus boycott in December 1955–56. This was more luck than judgement. The boycott was sparked by NAACP activist Rosa Parks challenging Montgomery's city bus segregation policy. Her arrest electrified the local black community. NAACP enlisted local black church leaders to help organise, inspire and finance a black bus boycott in protest at Parks' arrest. Twenty-six year old King happened to be one of Montgomery's church leaders. At the boycott's first meeting, he delivered a speech that revealed not only his oratorical gifts but also a political strategy – non-violent direct action. The two methods – direct action and NAACP litigation – effectively coalesced. NAACP got the courts to rule in favour of desegregated buses and after a year of boycott this was achieved in Montgomery in December 1956.

> This paragraph shows detailed knowledge of the situation in Montgomery in 1955–56 and also impressive powers of synthesis. It makes the point that King was *a* leader but not *the* leader in the bus boycott.

Following up this victory, King founded the Southern Christian Leadership Conference (SCLC) in 1957. Based in the black churches, SCLS led a series of campaigns in southern cities to expose the reality of racism. King invoked the Bible, the US Constitution and the American dream to support his stance – even though he declared in 1957 that he 'could never accommodate himself to capitalism'. Moving to Atlanta in 1960, he became co-pastor, along with his father, of Ebenezer Baptist Church. King did not initiate the student sit-in at an all-white Woolworth cafe in protest against segregation in Greensboro, North Carolina, in 1960. However, he supported the flood of sit-ins stand-ins and pray-ins that now took place across the South. King was imprisoned following a sit-in at an Atlanta cafe. Presidential candidate John F. Kennedy, anxious to solidify the black vote in the South, intervened to secure his release – proof of King's importance.

> This paragraph demonstrates an excellent understanding of King's role in 1957–60. The last sentence is powerful. King was an important figure.

But King remained just one of many black leaders. Indeed in 1961–62, he played a subordinate role in the continuing protests in the southern states. James Farmer's CORE organised the well-publicised 'freedom rides' on inter-state transport. Black student James Meredith challenged the segregated University of Mississippi, while the Student Non-Violent Co-ordinating Committee (SNCC) mobilised 50,000 students in scores of southern cities to participate in non-violent demonstrations. When SNCC mobilised students in Albany, Georgia, to protest against segregation and disfranchisement, King went along to support them in 1962. At Albany, he used a protest method that was to become his favourite – a peaceful march. His arrest did his cause no harm. Just the opposite: he used it to draw national attention to injustice in the South. He was able to make the point that in a 'free'

> This paragraph shows an ability to cut to the chase, focusing on key developments. It also continues the main theme. King was important but not the only leader of the civil rights movement.

country, which trumpeted its belief in freedom and democracy, a man could get arrested for participating in a protest march against discrimination and inequality.

In many respects, King's greatest success came in 1963. He first led a well-publicised black boycott of stores in Birmingham, Alabama, a bastion of southern racism. He also led protest marches. Birmingham's hot-headed police chief Bull Connor acted as King hoped he might, setting police dogs on black marchers and then using high-pressured water hoses on black children. King himself was imprisoned. He thus won the publicity he wanted. Most white Americans were appalled and amazed at what they saw on their TV sets. In August 1963, tens of thousands, blacks and whites, flocked to Washington D.C. for a civil rights rally at the Lincoln Memorial. Here King delivered his 'I have a dream' speech. If King was ever leader of the civil rights movement, this was the moment.

> A good paragraph which highlights King's importance. It provides evidence that the candidate's knowledge of events in 1963 is first rate.

The civil rights cause was ultimately supported by President Kennedy, who supported a comprehensive Civil Rights Bill which got bogged down in Congress. Kennedy's assassination enabled President Johnson to pass the measure. The 1964 Civil Rights Act enabled the federal government to end segregation in the South. It ended discrimination in public places, and provided more equal employment and educational opportunities in the South. Ironically, neither Kennedy nor Johnson rated or particularly respected King. They supported the civil rights cause – not King. King, who won the Nobel Peace Prize in 1964, remained active. The 1964 Act did not solve the problem of black disfranchisement. King's demonstrations, especially in Selma, Alabama, in 1965, did much to publicise the problem and to persuade Congress to pass the Voting Rights Act (1965), after which the numbers of black Americans voting in the South increased steadily.

> This is an important paragraph. It brings the chronological analysis to a compelling end and remains true to the position laid down in the introduction.

Thus King played a crucial role in the civil rights movement throughout the late 1950s and early 60s. A gifted orator and TV performer, he helped establish the non-violent strategy which won white opinion to the civil rights cause. If he did not make the civil rights movement, he played a vital role in its development. But he was just one of many black leaders, just as the SLCS was just one of many black protest movements. NAACP, CORE, SNCC and the National Urban League all played important roles. Their leaders did not attract the same media attention as King. But they were not necessarily led by him. Nor did all approve of his actions. The civil rights movement was far too amorphous to be led by one man. At its core were thousands of activists who campaigned for what they perceived to be right. Most admired King's actions and oratory but only a small number joined the SLCS. In that sense, King's influence was limited. But in many other ways, he proved an inspiring leader – *a* leader, not *the* leader.

> The conclusion does not disappoint. It pulls together the argument that was initiated in the introduction and developed throughout the essay. The last sentence sums up matters very nicely.

This is a Level 5 essay. It demonstrates detailed knowledge of a range of different issues. It also clearly engages with the question, offering a balanced and carefully reasoned argument which is sustained throughout the essay.

What makes a good answer?

Use this essay and the comments to make a bullet-pointed list of the characteristics of a Level 5 answer. Use this list when planning and writing your own practice essays.

The impact of the Roaring Twenties, Great Depression and New Deal on women

REVISED ☐

The Roaring Twenties

Women's position changed considerably after 1917.

The 19th Amendment

American women had long campaigned for the right to vote. In the late-nineteenth century several states had given women the vote. The female suffrage movement sprang back to life after 1912.

- The Women's Party, led by Alice Paul, copied the tactics of the British suffragettes, picketing the White House and deliberately provoking arrests, after which they went on hunger strikes.
- Carrie Chapman Catt, head of the National Suffrage Association, with a legacy of $1 million from Mrs Frank Leslie, publisher of *Leslie's Weekly*, organised a major campaign for female voting rights.

In 1918, the House of Representatives passed the 19th Amendment to the Constitution, which guaranteed women the vote in all US elections. It was pushed through the Senate in 1919. Ratification of the Amendment took another 14 months as states voted on the issue. But in 1920, the 19th Amendment was ratified. However, it did not result in a political revolution. Few women involved themselves in politics.

Equal Rights

Alice Paul and the Women's Party tried to advance female equality further by introducing an Equal Rights Amendment into Congress in 1923. This aimed to eliminate any remaining legal distinctions between genders. The proposed Amendment, however, failed to win Congressional approval.

Women's employment

The sharp increase in the number of women in the workforce during the First World War declined after 1919. Nevertheless, the USA's booming economy in the 1920s ensured that there was a steady increase in the number of employed women. This was more evolution than revolution. By 1900, women already had at least a token foothold in most occupations. In 1920, some 8.2 million found work outside the home. By 1930, this had risen to 10.4 million. Most were concentrated in traditional female occupations: domestic servants, office workers, teachers and dressmakers.

A new morality

Many young women enjoyed something of a revolution in lifestyle in the 1920s.

- More women spent their leisure time at dance halls, in cinemas and at sports clubs.
- Women's increased liberation was reflected in fashion. Corsets went out of fashion. Hemlines rose, hair became bobbed.
- Cosmetics became a growth industry.

Nevertheless, there were probably fewer 'flappers' – young women who adopted the latest crazes and fashions, with shorter hair and skirts – than the media suggested.

The Great Depression and the New Deal

The 1930s saw some changes in women's role.

Political change

In 1933, Roosevelt appointed Frances Perkins as secretary of labour. She was the first female cabinet member. But there were still few women in Congress.

Employment

The Depression caused the loss of women workers. Many employers felt that men should be employed ahead of women. Nevertheless, 13 million women were in work in 1940 – 2.5 million more than in 1930. Women's work was similar to what it had been in 1920.

Social

By the 1930s, the old code of marriage was changing. The old code had made the husband head and master of the family, while limiting the wife's sphere to the care of home and the children. By the 1930s, a code exalting love and companionship as the basis of marriage had gained ascendancy.

! Complete the paragraph ◀ a

Below are a sample exam question and a paragraph written in answer to this question. The paragraph contains a point and a concluding explanatory link back to the question, but lacks examples. Complete the paragraph by adding examples in the space provided.

To what extent did women's position in American society change in the years 1917–41?

By 1917, the female suffrage issue was very much back on the political agenda as a number of women's groups demanded the vote.

_____

_____

_____

Thus, by 1941 women had the vote but still had little real political power.

! Support or challenge?

Below is a sample exam-style question which asks you to what extent you agree with a specific statement. Below that is a list of general statements which are relevant to the question. Using your own knowledge and the information on the opposite page, decide whether these statements support or challenge the statement in question.

How far do you agree that women's position in the USA had changed massively in the years 1917–41?

STATEMENT	SUPPORT	CHALLENGE
Frances Perkins became secretary of labour in 1933.		
By 1940, 13 million women were in work.		
After 1920, women had more sexual independence.		
After 1920, cosmetics became an important industry.		
Flappers were fewer in number than the media suggested.		
Most American female workers were concentrated in traditional female occupations.		
The 19th Amendment ensured women the vote.		

The impact of the Second World War and suburban life on women, 1941–60

The Second World War

The need for female labour in the Second World War shook up old prejudices about gender roles.

Women's military role

Some 200,000 women served in the Women's Army Corps and the navy's equivalent, Women Accepted for Volunteer Emergency Service. Women were not expected to fight. But by serving as typists, drivers, telephonists, clerks and cooks, they released men for combat duty. Thousands of women also worked as nurses or female orderlies in field hospitals.

Women's employment

By 1945, over 6 million had entered the workforce – an increase of over 50 per cent since 1941. Old barriers fell as women entered employment of all kinds, becoming machinists, lumberjacks and railway track workers – occupations previously reserved for men. By 1944, women made up 14 per cent of all workers in shipbuilding and 40 per cent in aircraft plants. **Rosie the Riveter** symbolised women in war work. Her real counterparts performed so well in jobs once thought unsuitable for women that attitudes about women were altered.

In 1940, about 15 per cent of married women were employed outside the home. By 1945, nearly 25 per cent had found employment. In the workforce as a whole, married women outnumbered single women for the first time. In the 1930s, over 80 per cent of Americans opposed work by married women. By 1942, a poll showed 60 per cent in favour of employing married women in war industries.

The impact of suburban life, 1945–60

After 1945, women's role changed. The return of servicemen from the war had two main consequences:
- Women were encouraged – sometimes forced – to turn their wartime jobs over to returning veterans.
- There was a **baby boom**. The birth rate per 1,000 of total population grew from 19.4 in 1940 to over 24 per annum by 1946. This high rate did not decline until the 1960s.

The baby boom resulted in married women returning to their traditional housewife roles. However, given the fact that large families were costly to maintain, many married women sought employment. This was essential for poor families. But middle-class women, anxious to keep up with their neighbours, often sought part-time work.

Women tended to be discriminated against both in employment and in wages:
- Relatively few were in skilled crafts or the professions. Most went into low-paid, low-prestige occupations, such as clerical or **service industry** work.
- They were paid substantially less than men when doing the same work.

Women's place

The soaring birth rate reinforced the deeply embedded notion that woman's place was in the home. Having babies was seen as a major duty. Throughout the post-war era, teachers, politicians, churchmen and advertisers exalted the cult of domesticity, criticising the few feminists who tried to persuade women to broaden their horizons beyond crib and kitchen. Two social psychologists, Marynia Farnham and Ferdinand Lundberg, published a best-selling book in 1947, *Modern Woman: The Lost Sex,* in which they seemed to lend the authority of science to the view that women could achieve fulfilment only by accepting their natural functions as wives and mothers. Most middle-class women, living in new suburban housing estates, tried to conform to the ideal stereotype – marrying young, having at least four children, and being excellent wives and mothers.

Gender inequality

Gender inequality was enshrined in law and practice.
- 18 states refused to allow female jurors.
- 6 states did not allow women to enter into financial agreements without a male co-signatory.
- Many schools expelled pregnant students and fired pregnant teachers.

⊕ Develop the detail   **a**

Below are a sample exam question and a paragraph written in answer to this question. The paragraph contains a limited amount of detail. Annotate the paragraph to add additional detail to the answer.

> How accurate is it so say that the Second World War had a relatively limited impact on women's role in American society in the years 1941–60?

> Although women did a great deal of valuable war work, they quickly returned to their traditional roles after 1945. By 1950, most married women's place was in the home rather than at work, just as it had been before the war.

ⓘ Turning assertion into argument

Below are a sample exam-style question and a series of assertions. Read the exam question and then add a justification to each of the assertions to turn it into an argument.

> How far did women's position in American society change in the years 1941–60?

The need for more labour after 1941 had a significant impact on women's lives because . . .

_____

_____

'Rosie the Riveter' was an important symbol for women because . . .

_____

_____

The baby boom after 1945 had an important impact on women's lives because . . .

_____

_____

The book *Modern World: The Lost Sex* had an impact on women's lives because . . .

_____

_____

The emergence, achievements and limits of the women's liberation movement, 1961–80

Women's rights

The various 1960s liberation movements helped accelerate the emergence of a powerful women's rights crusade which challenged the 1950s cult of domesticity.

The impact of Betty Friedan

In 1963, **Betty Friedan** published *The Feminine Mystique*. Friedan claimed that a propaganda campaign, engineered by advertisers and women's magazines, had created the 'feminine mystique' of blissful domesticity, which had stifled women's potential. In Friedan's view, the middle-class home had become a 'comfortable concentration camp'. *The Feminine Mystique* was a best-seller. The book launched a new phase of female protest.

The National Organisation for Women (NOW)

In 1966, Friedan and a small group of activists founded NOW. Soon regarded as the NAACP of the women's movement, NOW grew rapidly. It spearheaded efforts to:
- end job discrimination on the basis of gender
- legalise abortions (which were illegal in 30 states)
- obtain federal and state support for childcare centres.

It used a variety of tactics including litigation, political pressure, public information campaigns and protests.

Women's Liberation

In the late 1960s, a women's liberation movement arose. Radical feminists opposed sexual oppression and cultural practices (like beauty contests) that objectified women. Women's 'lib' activists (like Jo Freeman) sought support through newsletters and '**consciousness-raising meetings**' aimed at raising awareness of gender inequalities and encouraging women to combat it. By 1974, two-thirds of women felt discriminated against (compared with only a quarter in 1960).

Congressional and Supreme Court action

In the early 1970s, Congress and the Supreme Court advanced the cause of gender equality.

- In 1972, colleges were required to institute 'affirmative action' programmes to ensure equal opportunities for women.
- In 1972, Congress approved the Equal Rights Amendment (ERA), which had been stuck in a House committee for almost 50 years (see page 48).
- The Supreme Court (in *Roe v Wade* in 1973) struck down state laws forbidding abortions during the first three months of pregnancy.

Sexual liberation

Changes in attitudes amounted to a sexual revolution in the 1960s with increased acceptance of casual premarital sex, abortion and extramarital relations. The pace of change was accelerated by the widespread availability of the first oral contraceptive for women (the 'pill') which liberated women from the fear of pregnancy. Liberals supported the greater freedom. Conservatives bemoaned the '**permissive society**'.

Success?

The women's movement was not entirely successful:
- By the late 1970s, divisions within the women's movement between moderate and radical feminists caused reform efforts to stagnate.
- The movement failed to broaden its appeal beyond the confines of the white middle class.
- ERA failed to get enough state support to become part of the Constitution.
- Many conservative men and women were opposed to feminism, blaming the rising divorce rate and the breakdown of the traditional family unit on feminists.
- NOW's successful efforts to change abortion laws generated a powerful reaction among Catholics and fundamentalist Protestants who mounted a powerful 'right to life' crusade.
- Few women were elected to Congress.
- Women still faced considerable discrimination on the employment front. Women's wages were 62 per cent those of men's in 1980. Women still held few top positions.

Achievements

By 1980, the women's movement's success seemed set to continue.

- Women constituted 51 per cent of the population. Their political power, only partially mobilised in the 1970s, had potential for achieving social change.
- Women's growing presence in the workforce assured them a greater share of economic and political influence. By the mid-1970s, over half of married women and nine out of ten female college graduates were employed outside the home. Many career women did not regard themselves as feminists. They worked because they and their families needed the money. Nevertheless, traditional gender roles changed to accommodate the two-career family. Differences between masculinity and femininity were disappearing as both genders took on the same roles at work.

Spectrum of importance

Below are a sample exam question and a list of general points, which could be used to answer the question. Use your own knowledge and the information on the opposite page to reach a judgement about the importance of these general points to the question posed. Write numbers on the spectrum below to indicate their relative importance. Having done this, write a brief justification of your placement, explaining why some of these factors are more important than others. The resulting diagram could form the basis of an essay plan.

How successful was the feminist movement in the years 1960–80?

1   The 1950s cult of domesticity

2   The influence of Betty Friedan

3   Discrimination in employment

4   The issue of abortion

5   The Equal Rights Amendment

6   Political involvement

Least important ←──────────────────────────────────→ Most important

You're the examiner

Below are a sample exam question and a paragraph written in answer to this question. Read the paragraph and the mark scheme provided on pages 109–10. Decide which level you would award the paragraph. Write the level below, along with a justification for your choice.

How far do you agree that there was need for a strong feminist movement in the USA in the years 1960–80?

One reason for the need of a strong feminist movement was the employment situation. By the mid-1960s, employment for middle-class women was becoming as normal as it had been for many years in poor and blue-collar families. However, most elite colleges, like Yale, either excluded women or segregated them. The top law schools, business schools and medical schools discouraged women applicants and admitted very few of them. The major corporations in the USA rarely hired women executives. Justification for such practices rested on the common assumption that women, biologically and emotionally, were fitted for and contented with domestic concerns — with caring for their children, husbands and housekeeping. In fact, millions of women were not contented. They resented the cult of domesticity. They also resented receiving less remuneration for the jobs they held than did men in equivalent positions. Something needed to be done to change matters.

Level:

Mark:

Reason for choosing this level and this mark:

_____

_____

Immigration in the 1920s

Many Americans opposed the huge influx of immigrants from eastern and southern Europe in the decades before 1914. This attitude continued after 1918.

The Red Scare

The Bolshevik Revolution in Russia in 1917 aroused fears of a new alien threat. Many were alarmed at the emergence of an American Communist movement, largely foreign-born in membership. A wave of industrial unrest in 1919 was widely interpreted as revolutionary (see page 16). Public opinion became strongly anti-immigrant.

Nativism

The flow of immigrants, slowed by the First World War, rose after 1919. From June 1920 to June 1921 over 800,000 people entered the USA, mostly from southern and eastern Europe. The rise of the Klan after 1915 (see page 28) was in part due to nativist concerns about immigration. The Klan concentrated much of its energies in trying to limit immigrant numbers. The foreign connections of so many radicals strengthened the sense that sedition was chiefly foreign-made. Many thought that immigrants were also responsible for criminal activity. This seemed confirmed in 1920 when two Italian-born anarchists, Nicola Sacco and Bartolomeo Vanzetti, were arrested for armed robbery and murder. After a trial conducted by a hostile judge, they were sentenced to death. The belief persists that they were sentenced for their beliefs and ethnic origins rather than for the crime they committed.

Immigration restriction

The surge in immigration and nativism brought an end to three centuries of unlimited immigration.

- In 1921, Congress passed the Emergency Immigration Act. This restricted new arrivals each year to 3 per cent of the foreign-born of any nationality, as shown in the 1910 census.
- The 1924 quota law reduced the number to 2 per cent based on the 1890 census, which included fewer of the 'new' immigrants. This law set a permanent limitation of slightly over 150,000 per year based on the 'national origins' of Americans in 1920. The purpose was to tilt the balance in favour of immigration from northern and western Europe, which was assigned about 85 per cent of the total. The law completely excluded people from Eastern Asia.

Western Hemisphere immigration

The quota law did not limit immigrants arriving from **Western Hemisphere** countries. Hispanics, chiefly Mexican and Puerto Rican, became the fastest-growing ethnic minority.

- Mexicans mainly settled in California and the Southwest. By the 1920s, Mexican migrants constituted 75 per cent of farm labour in the West. Farmers and growers treated Mexican workers almost as slaves, paying them extremely low wages. Other Mexicans found work in growing cities like Los Angeles and Tucson. Most Mexican immigrants were men. Many moved back and forth between their homeland and the USA, seeking available jobs.
- Puerto Rico had been an American possession since 1898. Its people were granted US citizenship in 1916. A surplus of labour (resulting from a shift from cotton to coffee production) led to Puerto Ricans moving to the USA – mainly to New York – in search of work.

Immigrant assimilation

Most new European immigrants remained loyal to their old roots. However, second generation immigrants, educated in American schools, tended to become typical and often model American citizens. Their American dream was like that of older-established Americans among whom they soon began to marry. Although initially low on the social scale, Italian and Jewish immigrants were perceived as 'white'. They were thus regarded – and regarded themselves – as superior to blacks.

Hispanic Americans, although officially regarded as 'white' by the US federal census, found it more difficult to assimilate, mainly because of the racism they faced. Many continued to live in their own communities well into the twentieth century – and beyond.

! Simple essay style

Below is a sample exam question. Use your own knowledge and the information on the opposite page to produce a plan for this question. Choose four general points, and provide three pieces of specific information to support each general point. Once you have planned your essay, write the introduction and conclusion for the essay. The introduction should list the points to be discussed in the essay. The conclusion should summarise the key points and justify which point was the most important.

How accurate is it to say that the principal reason for the limitation of immigrants to the USA was the result of racism in the years 1921–41?

! Mind map

Use the information on the opposite page to add detail (at least two points) to the mind map below.

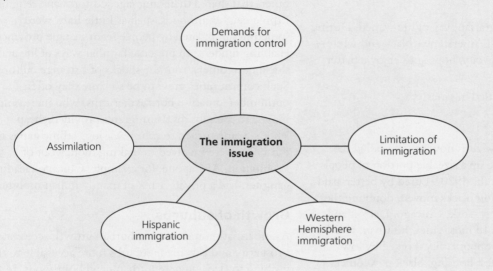

Demands for immigration control

Assimilation

The immigration issue

Limitation of immigration

Hispanic immigration

Western Hemisphere immigration

Urban development

The 1920 federal census revealed that for the first time, a majority of Americans lived in urban areas – defined as places with 2,500 or more people. The city thus became the focus of national experience. In addition to growth in metropolises like New York and Chicago, manufacturing led to expansion in dozens of regional centres, for example Birmingham (steel), Houston (oil) and Detroit (car production). Retail trades boosted growth in places like Minneapolis, Seattle and Atlanta. Warm-climate towns, for example, Miami and San Diego, also experienced huge expansion.

Urban incomers

- As cities grew, the agrarian way of life waned. During the 1920s, six million Americans – black and white – left their farms for the city, hoping to enjoy a better quality of life.
- Most immigrants settled in cities.

Black migration

African Americans, in what is now usually called the **Great Migration**, made up a sizeable portion of people on the move to cities in the 1920s. Lured by better-paid industrial jobs, 1.5 million blacks moved, doubling the black populations of New York, Chicago, Detroit and Houston in this decade. In most cities, however, racial discrimination blocked opportunity. Forced by low wages to seek the cheapest housing, black newcomers were forced into ghettos, like Chicago's South Side and New York's Harlem. Black efforts to move into white neighbourhoods sparked resistance. Fears of 'black invasion' prompted neighbourhood associations to adopt restrictive covenants, whereby white home owners pledged not to sell or rent property to blacks.

Hispanic migration

- In the 1920s, Mexican migrants crowded into low-rent districts in Southwestern cities like Denver and Los Angeles where they suffered poor sanitation, poor police protection and poor schools.
- The 1920s witnessed an influx of Puerto Ricans. Most Puerto Ricans moved to New York, attracted by contracts from employers seeking cheap labour. In the cities, they created *barrios* (communities) and found jobs in factories, hotels and domestic service. Puerto Ricans maintained traditional customs and developed businesses – grocery stores, cafes, boarding houses – and social organisations to help them adapt to American society.
- Successful Mexicans and Puerto Ricans – doctors, lawyers, business owners – became community leaders.

European immigrants

Most immigrants from southern and eastern Europe settled in America's largest cities. Here they lived with others that shared their language, customs and religion. Ethnic neighbourhoods, such as Little Italy, were sometimes populated by people from a single province, enabling residents to preserve familiar ways of life and shield newcomers from the shocks of a strange culture. Such communities grew to be so large they often outnumbered native-born Americans, who increasingly moved to the suburbs. Immigrants provided cheap labour. Some turned to crime. Various ethnic gangs in the 1920s were involved in making money out of Prohibition. Al Capone, for example, Chicago's leading gangster, had a private army of mainly Italian mobsters.

Growth of suburbs

As urbanisation increased, suburban growth accelerated. Prosperity and cars made suburbs more accessible to those wishing to flee congested urban neighbourhoods. In the 1920s, suburbs of Chicago, Cleveland and Los Angeles grew five to ten times faster than did the nearby central cities. Although some suburbs were industrial satellites, most provided homes for white middle-class communities. Increasingly, suburbs resisted annexation to core cities. Suburbanites, anxious to escape big-city crime, grime and taxes, fought to preserve control over their own police, schools and local services.

Mind map

Use the information on the opposite page to add detail (at least two points) to the mind map below.

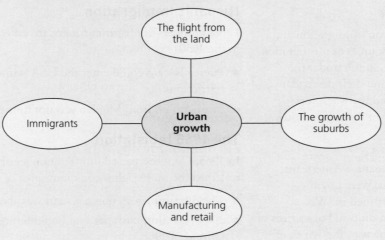

 Develop the detail

Below are a sample exam question and a paragraph written in answer to this question. The paragraph contains a limited amount of detail. Annotate the paragraph to add additional detail to the answer.

How accurate is it to say that the growth of American cities was mainly due to foreign immigrants in the years 1917–41?

There was widespread Hispanic migration into the USA in the years 1917 to 1941. Mexicans settled in cities in California and the Southwest. Puerto Ricans settled mainly in New York. Both groups tended to live within their own communities. In no city did they constitute a majority of the population.

The impact of the Second World War and government policy, 1941–80

The Second World War

The Second World War impacted on immigration and immigrants. It limited traditional sources of immigration. It also led to a campaign of national unity under the slogan 'America All'. Immigrants and their descendants, with very few exceptions, supported the war effort through military service and work in defence industries.

American Japanese

However, in 1942 some 112,000 Japanese Americans, who lived mainly on the west coast, were forcibly removed from their homes and confined in 'War Relocation Camps'. They were not disloyal but victims of fear and racial prejudice. During the war, thousands of Japanese Americans fought with distinction. Others served as interpreters and translators, the eyes and ears of US forces in the Pacific.

The situation in 1945

By 1945, 8 per cent of Americans were foreign-born – at that point in time the lowest percentage so far in the twentieth century. Despite the unity engendered by war, the nation was far from being a melting pot in which ethnic and religious differences had fused into a common 'American' nationality.

Government policy, 1945–80

The US government introduced several acts affecting would-be immigrants.

The McCarran-Walter Act, 1952

This act:
- allowed small quotas of immigrants from Asia
- eliminated 'race' as a barrier to naturalisation, enabling Asians to become American citizens
- maintained the existing 'national origins' system of immigration.

The act allowed more immigrants than was expected. For example, while only a few hundred Asians were allowed to enter the USA each year, family reunification provisions permitted some 45,000 Japanese and 32,000 Chinese to enter America in the 1950s.

Hispanic immigration

Large numbers of Hispanic Americans entered the USA in the 1950s.

- Puerto Ricans could enter the USA without restrictions.
- Immigration from Mexico was not limited by quotas.

The 1965 legislation

In 1965, Congress passed immigration legislation that reflected the more rights-conscious spirit of the era.

- The discriminatory quota system was abolished.
- 290,000 immigrants per year could be admitted to the USA as of 1968.
- Limits were placed on immigrants from Western Hemisphere countries: 120,000 per year were allowed with a maximum of 20,000 from any single nation.

The impact of the legislation

The new immigration law seemed unlikely to create major changes in the USA's demography. However, the law permitted the admission beyond numerical limits of close relatives of US citizens, both native-born and naturalised. Over the next decade an average of 100,000 were admitted each year, in addition to the 290,000 authorised.

After 1968, contrary to Congress' expectations, the flow of European immigrants declined and the numbers from Latin America and Asia began to swell. By 1976, more than half of the USA's legal immigrants came from Mexico, the Philippines, Korea, Cuba, Taiwan, India and the Dominican Republic. Because the birth rate of other Americans had stabilised, immigrants came to compose a steadily higher percentage of the population. By the late 1970s more than 450,000 legal immigrants arrived each year, fewer than a fifth of whom were Europeans. Thus by 1980, the number of foreign-born people had increased to 14 million as opposed to 9.7 million in 1960. Critics claimed that this strained schools and social services and deprived native-born Americans of jobs. Liberals argued that the immigrants brought valuable skills and contributed to economic growth and a richer ethno-cultural mix.

Establish criteria

Below is a sample exam-style question which requires you to make a judgement. The key term in the question has been underlined. Defining the meaning of the key term can help you establish criteria that you can use to make a judgement.

Read the question, define the key term and then set out two or three criteria based on the key term, which you can use to reach and justify a judgement.

To what extent did the USA experience <u>mass immigration</u> in the years 1941–80?

Definition:

_____

_____

Criteria to judge the extent to which the USA experienced mass immigration in the years 1941–80:

_____

_____

_____

_____

Reach a judgement

Having defined the key term and established a series of criteria, you should now make a judgement. Consider how far the USA experienced mass immigration according to each criterion. Summarise your judgements below:

Criterion 1:

_____

Criterion 2:

_____

Criterion 3:

_____

Criterion 4:

_____

Finally, sum up your judgement. Based on the criteria, how accurate is it to say that the USA experienced mass immigration in the years 1941–80?

_____

_____

_____

_____

The social impact of cinema, popular music and the radio, 1917–45

Impact of the cinema

Cinema-going, popular before the First World War, became even more popular after 1917.

Hollywood

By 1917, Hollywood had become synonymous with the film industry – an industry which was still 'silent'. During the 1920s a few major companies controlled production, distribution and exhibition. Producing around 600 films per year, the movie industry organised its output around genres such as westerns, romance or comedy. Stars like Charlie Chaplin, Buster Keaton and Rudolph Valentino became world famous.

Talkies

The first movie with a sound accompaniment was *Don Juan* (1926), but the success of talking pictures was established by *The Jazz Singer* (1927) starring Al Jolson.

Cinema's Golden Age

By the 1930s, movies were the chief mass entertainment of Americans. Sound fostered verbal comedy, musicals and crime films as new genres. Filmmakers such as Frank Capra and John Ford shaped cultural and historical myths. Two colour films of 1939 – *Gone with the Wind* and *The Wizard of Oz* – were among the most popular movies ever made.

The Second World War

During the war, the film industry was seen as vital to national morale. It functioned as usual, with some supervision over content by the Office of War Information. Cinema audiences soared during the war, reaching their all-time high in 1946.

The impact of popular music

Even before 1917, the USA had a huge influence on worldwide popular music and dance.

Jazz

After the success of the Original Dixieland Jazz Band in New York in 1917, black jazz musicians found themselves in demand in the North. Prohibition brought **speakeasies** during the 1920s, many of which hired jazz musicians to attract customers. Dances such as the Charleston and the Black Bottom became popular. Although conservatives viewed jazz as a threat to traditional values, it continued to rise in popularity. Louis Armstrong and Duke Ellington became big stars.

Radio's influence

Radio brought music to more consumers and stimulated the sale of sheet music and phonograph records. It helped the rise of 'crooners' like Bing Crosby.

Broadway

The 1920s was a golden age for Broadway musicals. Songwriters such as Irving Berlin, Cole Porter and Richard Rodgers wrote for the musical stage.

Swing

Swing dominated the jazz scene from 1935–45. Benny Goodman's orchestra is credited with launching the swing craze and the big-band era. By the late 1930s, hundreds of dance bands were playing in hotels, ballrooms and nightclubs. As the swing era progressed, band vocalists such as Frank Sinatra became stars in their own right.

Impact of the radio

The broadcast by station KDKA in Pittsburgh on 2 November 1920 is regarded as the birth of American broadcasting. Operated by the Westinghouse Corporation to encourage purchase of its radios, KDKA offered a weekly schedule of talk and music. As public interest soared, some 500 stations were on air by 1922. Selling 'time' to advertisers quickly became the accepted means of meeting operating costs.

Despite the Great Depression, radio prospered. By the 1930s, popular formats were well established. They included situation comedies, variety and music programmes, newscasts, daytime serial dramas and evening dramas of many kinds. Radio stars ranked in public appeal with those of film and stage. Roosevelt used radio 'fireside chats' in the 1930s to 'sell' his New Deal measures. Radio's share of all advertising soared – from under 1 per cent in 1928 to 15 per cent in 1945. By 1945, there were over 1,000 radio stations.

Introducing an argument

Below are an exam question, an essay plan and a basic introduction and conclusion. Rewrite the introduction and conclusion so that they contain an argument about the impact of radio on the USA's music industry in the years 1920–45.

To what extent did radio revolutionise the American music industry in the years 1920–45?

Key points

- The music industry pre-1920.
- The development of radio.
- Popular music in the period.
- The impact of radio on popular music.

Introduction

Radio's influence on America's music industry was massive. Radio broadcasts began in the USA in 1920. From the start, radio shows played a considerable amount of music of all kinds. The choice of music played had a huge influence on Americans' musical taste.

Conclusion

In conclusion, radio promoted 'popular' music and the careers of singers like Bing Crosby. However, Americans continued to go to dances, concerts and shows so radio was just one influence on musical tastes.

Eliminate irrelevance

Below are a sample exam question and a paragraph written in answer to this question. Read the paragraph and identify parts of the paragraph that are not directly relevant to the question. Draw a line through the information that is irrelevant and justify your deletions in the margin.

How accurate is it to say that cinema dominated American culture in the years 1917–45?

Cinema, popular before the First World War, became even more popular in the 1920s. Hollywood, a Los Angeles suburb, became synonymous with the film industry and American movie culture. It offered film-makers more sunlight, more varied terrain and lower wage scales than elsewhere. During the 1920s Hollywood perfected a so-called studio system, with a few major companies controlling the bulk of production, distribution and exhibition. Producing around 600 films each year, the industry organised its output around stars and genres. Films were sold and promoted on the basis of their star performers and genre category, such as western, mystery, horror, romance or comedy. The comedies of Harold Lloyd, Buster Keaton and Charlie Chaplin remain classics. Stars like Greta Garbo and Rudolph Valentino became public icons who embodied Hollywood glamour and screen romance. Promoted as 'every woman's dream', Valentino died at the age of 31, soon after his hospitalisation for a perforated ulcer. His sudden death prompted an outpouring of grief from his legions of fans. The mid-1920s saw the introduction of synchronised recorded sound directly onto the celluloid film strip. The first movie with a sound accompaniment was *Don Juan* (1926) but the success of talking pictures was established by *The Jazz Singer* (1927) starring Al Jolson. Sound fostered verbal comedy, musicals and crime films as new genres. By 1930 movies were the chief mass entertainment of Americans. Cinema thus had a huge cultural influence and its 'golden age' still lay ahead.

The TV boom

In 1948, only 172,000 homes had TVs. Few Americans could afford a set. The boom came as prices fell. By 1952, 15.3 million homes had TVs. By 1955, there were 32 million sets – 75 per cent of all households. By 1960, 90 per cent of households had black and white sets. Colour sets became affordable in the 1960s. By 1970, 38 per cent of homes had colour TVs. By 1980, the vast majority of homes had colour. They also had scores of channels to watch.

Popular programmes

Initially (until 1952) TV seemed aimed at people with high-brow tastes, if only because most viewers were well off and highly educated. But once TV took off, sponsors insisted on shows that appealed to mass audiences. Millions of families abandoned other activities to watch early stars such as the comedians Milton Berle and Lucille Ball. By the late 1950s, pre-recorded series dominated TV prime time, among them popular westerns such as *Gunsmoke* and detective series such as *77 Sunset Strip*. The quest for mass audiences (to attract advertisers) led networks like CBS and NBC to sponsor general-interest programmes. The *Ed Sullivan Show* attracted huge audiences in the late 1950s. Cartoons and quiz shows were also popular. By the 1960s, polls reported that TV was the favourite leisure activity of nearly half the population. Most Americans watched TV for more than three hours a day.

TV's bias

TV executives and producers in the 1950s and 60s tried not to offend people. To a large extent they were dependent on advertising for their revenue. TV producers catered carefully to sponsors (such as cigarette companies) and worked hard to reflect perceived norms.

- Businessmen and professional people were favourably portrayed.
- Few programmes in the 1950s featured black Americans (unless they were servants or domestic workers) as main characters.
- Political issues were mainly off limits. So was frankness about sex.
- Fathers tended to be all-knowing, mothers all-supportive (and at home) and children generally obedient and loveable.

The impact of TV

Debates over the cultural influence of TV, which began in the 1950s, continued for many more decades. Those who argued that TV's power was large – and harmful – claimed that TV:

- strengthened violent tendencies in people
- sabotaged the reading habit
- stifled conversation
- induced a general passivity of mind
- harmed radio, newspapers, magazines and cinema
- gave enormous boosts to the advertising industry.

Other observers were more positive. They claimed that TV was hardly all-powerful. TV viewers were far from passive. They argued heatedly about the meaning of what they had seen. Moreover, commercials did not sweep all before them. Millions of Americans smoked and bought large cars before the rise of TV commercials.

TV analysts claimed that Americans looked at the 'texts' of TV as they did other aspects of mass culture, in highly individualised ways. Viewers were not passive receptacles. They made choices. The class, gender, religion and ethnicity of people affected responses.

Arguably, TV helped to develop and define a more national culture. As the networks sent out nationwide programmes (and commercials), they may have helped to standardise tastes and to diminish regional and social division. Interestingly, however, millions of viewers remained stubbornly attached to regional, ethnic or racial subcultures and resisted aspects of the homogenised 'outside world' that TV thrust at them.

Develop the detail

Below are a sample exam question and a paragraph written in answer to this question. The paragraph contains a limited amount of detail. Annotate the paragraph to add additional detail to the answer.

To what extent did television come to dominate American entertainment and leisure time in the years 1950–70?

In 1950, nine out of ten American homes had a radio. Fewer than one in ten homes had a television. This soon changed. By 1960, more than nine out of ten homes had television sets. By 1970, television had replaced radio as the dominant provider of American entertainment.

 ## Identify key terms

Below is a sample exam question which includes a key word or term. Key terms are important because their meaning can be helpful in structuring your answer, developing an argument and establishing criteria that will help form the basis of a judgement.

To what extent did television affect American culture in the years 1950–70?

- First, identify the key word or term. This will be a word or phrase that is important to the meaning of the question. Underline the word or phrase.
- Secondly, define the key phrase. Your definition should set out the key features of the phrase or word that you are defining.
- Third, make an essay plan that reflects your definition.
- Finally, write a sentence answering the question that refers back to the definition.

Now repeat the task, and consider how the change in key terms affects the structure, argument and final judgement of your essay.

To what extent did television affect American values and beliefs in the years 1950–70?

The impact of radio

Before radio, newspapers provided Americans with news of current affairs. Although newspapers continued to be powerful throughout the inter-war years (and thereafter), by the 1930s radio was reducing their influence. By the late 1930s, virtually 80 per cent of the population had radio and listened to it on average four hours per day. While tuning in mainly for entertainment, Americans listened to news reports and current affairs programmes. President Roosevelt was good at using the radio. His so-called 'fireside chats', which explained his New Deal programmes, were highly effective.

TV news reporting

Initially news programmes lost money and the TV networks offered them mainly to placate federal overseers. Evening news reports lasted only 15 minutes. However, by the 1960s TV news had gained respect and larger audiences.

- In 1963, CBS and NBC expanded their nightly newscasts to 30 minutes.
- By 1963, most surveys suggested that Americans ranked TV as their main source of news/information.
- CBS News scored a ratings coup in the late 1970s with its top-rated *60 Minutes,* an hour-long collection of features and interviews dubbed a TV 'news magazine'. For the first time, a news programme successfully competed for audiences in evening prime time.
- Early morning news programmes became popular in the 1970s.

The impact of TV

TV had a huge impact on the way Americans interpreted events in the USA and the world.

The 1950s

TV brought important events into people's homes.

- In 1952, vice presidential candidate Nixon, accused of financial corruption, used national television to defend himself. His so-called **'Checkers' speech** impressed Americans and he remained on the Republican ticket.
- As many as 29 million viewers watched President Eisenhower's inauguration in 1953.
- In 1954, the Army-McCarthy hearings in the Senate were televised, exposing McCarthy as a truculent bully.

The 1960 presidential debates

In 1960, presidential candidates Kennedy and Nixon took part in three televised debates. Nixon was ahead in the polls before the first debate. Those who heard the debate on radio thought he had won. But those who watched on TV – over 60 million people – thought Kennedy had won. He went on to win the 1960 election. TV helped advance the careers of telegenic politicians like Kennedy and Reagan.

Civil Rights

TV cameras captured the events at Little Rock (1957), at Birmingham (1963), at Selma (1965) and a host of other occasions when violence was used against peaceful civil rights activists. Images of events in the South amazed and angered viewers all over the USA, assisting the civil rights cause.

The Vietnam War

Television news coverage of the Vietnam War – the USA's first 'living room war' – is often regarded as crucial in determining its outcome by turning US opinion against the war. However, TV coverage up to 1968 was, with few exceptions, supportive of the war. Fearful of upsetting viewers, the networks rarely showed actual combat or bloodshed. Nevertheless, by 1968 news reporting of the conflict was more critical and some disturbing scenes (in colour) found their way into Americans' homes. This probably accentuated an already widespread conviction that the war had no clear goals and was going badly.

A limited impact?

The influence of network news should not be overstated. The nightly national newscasts never had audiences comparable to the entertainment shows. Local newscasts usually had larger followings. They usually focused on light features and sensational crimes.

! Complete the paragraph   a

Below are a sample exam-style question and a paragraph written in answer to this question. The paragraph contains a point and a concluding explanatory link back to the question, but lacks examples. Complete the paragraph by adding examples in the space provided.

> How accurate is it to say that television reporting dominated Americans' perception of news in the years 1950–80?

In 1950, relatively few Americans had televisions. Moreover, news reporting was relatively slow to develop in the 1950s. Initially, news programmes lost money and news reports lasted only 15 minutes. Nevertheless, it was soon clear that television could bring important events into people's homes.

_____

_____

_____

Thus, by 1960 television had become a major force in the way Americans received the news.

! Support or challenge?

Below is a sample exam-style question which asks you to what extent you agree with a specific statement. Below that is a list of general statements which are relevant to the question. Using your own knowledge and the information on the opposite page, decide whether these statements support or challenge the statement in question.

> How accurate is to say that television news reporting determined the way most Americans understood events in the USA and the world in the years 1950–80?

STATEMENT	SUPPORT	CHALLENGE
Radio news reporting remained influential.		
Entertainment programmes were more popular than news programmes.		
Surveys indicated that most Americans (by 1963) regarded TV as their main source of news.		
Local newscasts were more popular than national newscasts.		
TV reporting of the Vietnam War was influential in determining its outcome.		
Newspapers continued to provide Americans with much of their news.		
The 1960 televised presidential debates probably determined the outcome of the election.		

Exam focus

Below is a sample essay. Read it and the comments around it.

To what extent were the lives of American women dominated by the 'cult of domesticity' in the years 1945–63?

During the Second World War, large numbers of American women entered the workforce. Given that millions of men were needed in the USA's armed forces, women's labour was necessary if America was to be the arsenal of democracy. Women responded in huge numbers. Rosie the Riveter symbolised women in war work. Her real counterparts performed so well in jobs once thought only suitable for men that old prejudices about gender roles in the workplace were challenged. The end of the war, however, saw a return to 'normalcy'. Most women returned to their traditional roles. For two decades the 'cult of domesticity' – the notion that women's place was in the home – held considerable sway. The 'cult' was not as pervasive as it had once been. Many women – single and married – remained in the workforce after 1945 – so many that domesticity was only part of women's lives. Nevertheless, as this essay will show, the 'cult of domesticity' very much extended beyond the home to the work place.

By 1945, a quarter of American married women were in gainful employment. In the workforce as a whole, married women for the first time outnumbered single women. Many worked in defence jobs. These jobs were the ones most vulnerable to post-war cuts. The return of millions of servicemen also endangered women's employment. Unions ensured that they were eased out of jobs traditionally done by men. It should be said that many women were pleased to give up their jobs. War work had not been a wonderful experience for all – perhaps even most – women. One reason why so many willingly handed over their work tools was the post-war baby boom. The population soared after 1945, the boom continuing until the 1960s. The soaring birth rate reinforced the deeply embodied notion that a woman's place was in the home as tender of the hearth and guardian of the children. Having children, moreover, was seen as American women's duty – just as war work had been.

Consequently, women returned to their traditional role. They were encouraged to do so by educators, politicians, church ministers, advertisers and the media – particularly women's magazines and television (by the early 1950s). Peer group pressure was also a powerful force. Women were encouraged to forget wartime generated thoughts of their own career in the workplace. 'Back to the kitchen' was the repeated refrain. Women were constantly told that no job was more necessary or more rewarding than that of housewife and mother. Two social psychologists, Marynia Farnham and Ferdinand Lundberg, published a best-selling book in 1947 entitled *Modern Woman: The Lost Sex*, in which they seemed to lend the authority of science to the view that women could achieve fulfilment only by accepting their natural functions as wives and mothers. Adlai Stevenson, the liberal Democrat presidential candidate, told Smith College graduates in 1955 that their heroic purpose in life was to 'influence man and boy' in the 'humble role of housewife'.

It was difficult to challenge the view that women's place was in the home. The media produced a stereotypical role model. A special issue of *Life* magazine in 1956, for example, featured the 'ideal' middle-class woman. She was 32 years old, a suburban housewife, 'pretty and popular', a mother of four who had married at the age of 16. She was depicted as an excellent wife, mother, hostess, volunteer and 'home manager' who made her own clothes, hosted dozens of dinner parties each year, sang in the church choir, worked with the school PTA and was devoted to her husband. According to *Life*, her daily life revolved around attending clubs or charity meetings, driving the children to school, shopping, exercising and pursuing

---

This introduction starts confidently. It goes on to focus on the set question and provides a guide of the likely direction the essay will take. The suggestion, in the last sentence, that it intends to broaden the definition of the 'cult of domesticity' is interesting – and valid.

A well-informed paragraph which establishes the situation in 1945 and two of the developments which resulted in women returning to the home.

This paragraph examines the pressures on women to conform to society's expectations. It displays good knowledge and the Stevenson quote is effective.

This paragraph is effective. It describes what the 'cult of domesticity' actually meant. The last two sentences hopefully point the way to women's role outside the home.

a hobby. Such was the ideal. It should be said that this was not necessarily the reality of most women's lives. The reality was that many women did actually leave the house to work.

Single women were expected to work – and did. Poor married women had little option but to work to provide support for their families. In the South, many poor blacks were domestic servants. They did housework for rich white women as well as their own housework – the real 'cult of domesticity'. But middle-class women also took jobs (often part time) in the 1950s. This was to ensure they could maintain their affluent lifestyles and keep up with their neighbours by purchasing new luxury goods and gadgets. These gadgets often made housework easier, ensuring women had more free time. Unfortunately, women lacked economic equality. By 1963, most remained in low-paid jobs such as waitresses, cleaners, shop assistants or secretaries. Educated women were expected to choose 'female occupations' such as nursing and teaching, which conformed to traditional stereotypes of women as nurturers and carers. They rarely rose to top positions. In the early 1960s, for example, women constituted 80 per cent of teachers but only 10 per cent were heads. Only 7 per cent of doctors and 3 per cent of lawyers were women. Arguably, this discrimination within the workforce was another aspect of the cult of domesticity. Women were seen as very different to men, operating within different 'spheres' and having different priorities. Accordingly, within the workforce they were treated as second-class citizens.

This paragraph displays good skills of analysis and synthesis. It also displays good knowledge. The final three sentences are perceptive and link back to a claim in the introduction.

In 1963, Betty Friedan, a Smith College graduate and suburban housewife, drew attention to the dissatisfaction of many middle-class housewives. In *The Feminine Mystique* she claimed that women were imprisoned in a 'comfortable concentration camp', focusing on the needs of their children and husband rather than on their own needs. Friedan urged women to break out of the 'camp' and fulfil their potential through education and work. Her best-selling book tapped a reservoir of discontent, especially among female college students, and is usually seen as launching the women's rights movement.

Friedan is worth mentioning – given that the time period in the question extends to 1963. It provides some indication of what happened next – no bad thing.

In conclusion, there is no doubt that the cult of domesticity had considerable force in the decade and a half after 1945. Most women knew their 'place' and that place was in the home. Most tried to live up to society's expectations. By no means all were dissatisfied with their lot. Probably more women opposed Friedan and the women's rights movement in the mid-1960s than supported her/it. Many had no desire to work: they were happy at home, just as many women had been delighted to return to the home after 1945. But some were unhappy and angry. They did not like domesticity. Nor did they like the fact that they faced discrimination within the work force. And many were frustrated by the demands of effectively holding two full-time jobs – unpaid housekeeper and underpaid service worker. American women were by no means confined to the home after 1945. But the 'cult of domesticity' – a 'cult' which saw women as far from equal to men – extended to the workforce. In that sense, the 'cult' very much dominated women's lives after 1945.

The conclusion very much ties in with the introduction and with the issues raised in the course of the essay. It displays consistent analysis.

This essay achieves a mark in Level 5. It is thorough and detailed, clearly engaging with the question and offering a balanced and carefully reasoned argument which is sustained throughout the essay. It also shows good skills of analysis and synthesis.

Consolidation

This is a long and detailed essay. Arguably it is overlong. Without losing the overall argument of the essay, experiment with reducing its length by 100 words. This is a particularly useful exercise for trying to produce an essay which gets to the heart of the question without being overlong.

Boom, bust and recovery, 1917–41 REVISED

Boom, 1921–29

Once the brief depression of 1919–21 was over, America entered an era of unparalleled prosperity.

Increase in productivity

The key to the boom was a great increase in productivity resulting from technological innovation. While the population increased by 16 per cent during the 1920s, industrial production almost doubled. The US chemicals industry did well, particularly in the manufacture of synthetic textiles and plastics. The electricity industry did even better: electricity consumption more than doubled in the 1920s.

The automobile industry

The automobile industry contributed a great deal to the business boom. Henry Ford, by adapting assembly-line techniques and concentrating on a standardised model, the Model T, brought the car to the masses. By 1925, he was producing a car every ten seconds. There was competition from other manufacturers, notably General Motors and Chrysler, who offered more stylish models. By 1929, there were nearly 27 million cars – one car for every five Americans. In 1929, the car industry employed 450,000 workers – 7 per cent of all manufacturing wage-earners. The automobile industry stimulated other industries – steel, rubber, oil, road building and service stations.

Bust, 1929–33

In October 1929, the value of stocks and shares on Wall Street collapsed. This crash was followed by the most devastating economic collapse in US history. Business confidence evaporated as bankruptcies and bank failures multiplied. US trade fell from $10 billion in 1929 to $3 billion in 1932. By mid-1932, industrial output had dropped to half the 1929 level. In early 1929, 1.5 million were unemployed – 3 per cent of the workforce. By December 1932, unemployment was over 12 million – 25 per cent of the workforce. Farmers also suffered as food prices collapsed.

Recovery, 1933–41

In 1932, Roosevelt became president. He promised 'bold persistent experimentation' to get America out of the Depression. His New Deal measures had some success.

The situation in 1934

By 1934, Roosevelt had halted the banking panic, created new institutions to reconstruct industry and farming, authorised the largest public works programme in American history, set up the TVA and set aside millions of dollars for relief to the unemployed. But real economic recovery proved elusive. Around 11 million people were still jobless in mid-1934.

The situation in 1937–39

Roosevelt was re-elected in 1936 – proof that most Americans believed that Roosevelt's measures were working. In mid-1937, US output surpassed that of 1929. Roosevelt now tried to balance the budget by cutting government spending. This sent the economy into reverse. Indeed, the rate of decline in 1937–38 was sharper than it had been in 1929. Industrial production fell by a third and national income by a tenth. By 1938, 11.5 million workers were unemployed. In 1938, Roosevelt asked Congress for $3.75 billion for relief and public works. Congress obliged and by the summer the economy had begun a slow upward climb. The New Deal thus brought only partial recovery. The USA was less successful at reducing unemployment than Germany or Britain. Some 10 million Americans – 17 per cent of the workforce – were still unemployed in 1939.

The situation by 1941

The USA benefited from the outbreak of war in Europe in 1939. US businesses broke into markets previously dominated by European manufacturers. After 1940 there were more jobs as the US government began to prepare for war. Nevertheless, unemployment remained high until America went to war in 1941.

Spectrum of importance

Below are a sample exam question and a list of general points which could be used to answer the question. Use your own knowledge and the information on the opposite page to reach a judgement about the importance of these general points to the question posed. Write numbers on the spectrum below to indicate their relative importance. Having done this, write a brief justification of your placement explaining why some of these factors are more important than others. The resulting diagram could form the basis of an essay plan.

> To what extent was big business responsible for the USA's good and bad economic times in the years 1921–41?

1 The 1920s boom

2 Government's pro-business policies in the 1920s

3 The Wall Street Crash

4 The Great Depression

5 World economic conditions

6 The New Deal

7 US economic recovery, 1933–39

8 US economic recovery, 1939–41

◄───►

Least important   Most important

ⓘ You're the examiner

Below are a sample exam question and a paragraph written in answer to this question. Read the paragraph and the mark scheme provided on pages 109–10. Decide which level you would award the paragraph. Write the level below, along with a justification for your choice.

> How far do you agree that the New Deal transformed the USA's economy in the years 1933–41?

Far from transforming the US economy, it is possible to claim that the New Deal was neither new nor, more importantly, very successful. At best it brought about only partial recovery. The USA was less successful at reducing unemployment in the 1930s than Germany or Britain. In no year after 1933 did the unemployment rate fall below 14 per cent. Some 10 million Americans — 17 per cent of the workforce — were still out of work in 1939. Not until 1941 would full employment and prosperity return, and only then because of the Second World War and rearmament. The New Deal work programmes were inefficient, doing little to enhance skills. WPA (Works Progress Administration), for example, became known as 'We Piddle Around'. There was also limited social reform. Many groups were excluded from pensions and unemployment insurance. The poor remained poor. Arguably the New Deal agencies simply got in the way of recovery, and whatever economic success there was occurred despite the New Deal policies, not because of them.

Level:

Mark:

Reason for choosing this level and this mark:

_____

_____

The impact of the Second World War and post-war growth, 1941–69

The Second World War

The war accomplished what the New Deal had not – the rescue of the economy.

Boom

- By 1944, unemployment was down to 670,000 – 1.2 per cent.
- The personal income of farmers more than doubled between 1940–45.
- Business profits rose from $6 billion in 1939 to $10.5 billion in 1945.
- The war led to co-operation between government and big business. Business accepted that the government had a role to play in managing the economy. The government, in turn, accepted that it needed business to come up with the goods – which it did on a huge scale.
- Between 1940 and 1945, American industry produced over 100,000 tanks, 300,000 aircraft and 93,000 ships. By 1944, the USA was producing twice as much as Germany, Japan and Italy combined.

The situation in 1945

By 1945 the USA was the world's richest nation. It had a population of 140 million people – 7 per cent of the world's population. It produced 50 per cent of the world's manufacturing output and 42 per cent of the world's income. **Per capita** income was twice that of its nearest competitors.

Post-war affluence and growth, 1945–60

The economy continued to boom after 1945.

Reasons for economic growth

- The USA emerged from the Second World War in a far better economic shape than its potential rivals.
- Americans had saved money during the war and wanted to spend it on commodities that had been scarce during the war.
- US industry and transportation benefited from cheap oil.
- Ever-increasing investment in research and development led to scientific and technological advances that increased productivity.
- There was a baby boom after 1945. This encouraged the purchase of homes and children's goods.

Growth areas

The greatest growth areas were advertising, aviation, cars, chemicals, construction, defence, electronics, food processing, pharmaceuticals, soft drinks and tobacco. As a result, America's **GNP** rose from $355.3 billion in 1950 to $487.76 billion in 1960.

Construction

Thirteen million new homes were built in the period 1948–58. This construction boom provided employment and encouraged a spate of other industries.

The automobile industry

The car industry employed hundreds of thousands of workers. Most cars on American roads by the 1950s were manufactured in Detroit by the Big Three – General Motors, Ford and Chrysler. In 1955, 7.9 million cars were manufactured.

Service industries

The growing use of cars led to the proliferation of motels, fast-food outlets and out-of-town shopping malls. This contributed to increased numbers of service workers, such as petrol station attendants and waitresses.

Decline of blue-collar workers

By 1960, the 7.6 million service workers and 21.2 million white-collar workers outnumbered the 25.6 million manual workers (blue-collar workers). Growing automation decreased the need for labour in factories and mines.

The 1960s

Economic prosperity continued into the 1960s.

Kennedy's presidency

During Kennedy's presidency, GNP expanded by 20 per cent and industrial production by 22 per cent, while personal income rose by 15 per cent. However:

- there were slowdowns of economic growth in 1961 and 1962
- Kennedy was concerned about the USA's international balance of payments deficit.

Johnson's presidency

For most of Johnson's presidency, the economy continued to boom. However, by 1968–69 there were growing problems.

- The 1967 trade deficit of nearly $4 billion was three times that of 1966.
- The US began to suffer from inflation and rising consumer prices.
- There was no rise in industrial production.

The challenges of the 1970s are covered on page 76.

Simple essay style

Below is a sample exam question. Use your own knowledge and the information on the opposite page to produce a plan for this question. Choose four general points, and provide three pieces of specific information to support each general point. Once you have planned your essay, write the introduction and conclusion for the essay. The introduction should list the points to be discussed in the essay. The conclusion should summarise the key points and justify which point was the most important.

How accurate is it to say that the USA enjoyed economic boom and prosperity in the years 1941–69?

Complete the paragraph

Below are a sample exam question and a paragraph written in answer to this question. The paragraph contains a point and specific examples, but lacks a concluding analytical link back to the question. Complete the paragraph adding this link in the space provided.

How far was the Second World War responsible for the USA's economic success in the years 1941–69?

The USA's economy had proved its strength in the Second World War. It continued to prove its strength thereafter. The USA was fortunate that most of its main economic competitors – Britain, Germany, France, Japan – had suffered considerable economic damage during the war. It would take them several years to recover. The USA, by contrast, emerged from the war in a much better shape. In 1945 the USA, with 140 million people, had 7 per cent of the world's population but 42 per cent of the world's income and over 50 per cent of the world's manufacturing output. Its per capita income was twice that of any other country. Most Americans had saved money during the war and wished to spend it on commodities that had been scarce during the war. Moreover, many reunited husbands and wives and newly married couples were keen to start families. The result was a baby boom that was to continue for over a decade. This encouraged demand for bigger houses and more consumer goods. In consequence,

_____

_____

_____

Fluctuations in the standard of living, 1917–41

Prosperity, 1917–29

For most Americans, the standard of living increased during the 1920s.

The consequences

Prosperity benefited most industrial workers. Hours of work declined, real wages increased by a third and there was little unemployment. Many employers extended recreational facilities, and introduced life insurance and pension plans. Many Americans could afford to buy radios, new houses and cars, and go to the cinema and watch sport. Within the domestic sphere, women became more independent as electrical appliances and processed foods freed them from much drudgery. They also bore fewer children. Birth control, increasingly practised despite statutory obstacles, brought down the birth rate and gave women more control over their lives.

The less fortunate

Not all Americans enjoyed a higher standard of living.

- Textile workers and coal miners did not see wages rise.
- Decline in foreign demand after 1920 led to a drastic fall in farm prices. Many farmers, especially in the South and Midwest, lived in poverty.
- Blacks remained the poorest social group.

Depression, 1929–33

The Depression had a major impact on standards of living. By late 1932, 12 million Americans were unemployed. There was no dole and private charity was unable to cope with the scale of the emergency. Millions of people roamed the countryside, stealing rides on freight trains and looking for work. Others congregated on the outskirts of cities in shanty towns known as Hoovervilles. It was not just the unemployed who suffered.

- Those lucky enough to be in full time work saw their average weekly earnings fall by a third.
- Many people were only employed part time.
- Farmers' incomes plummeted as farm prices collapsed.

Recovery, 1933–41

Roosevelt's New Deal measures brought about something of an economic recovery. More Americans managed to find work. Roosevelt also introduced a number of measures which helped those in need.

- The Federal Emergency Relief Act (1933) ensured that federal money could be provided for direct relief. Instead of putting people on the dole, the government tried to provide jobs, for example, repairing roads, improving schools and maintaining playgrounds.
- The Works Progress Administration (1935) provided even more work relief. During its eight-year history, it employed 8.5 million people and spent $11 billion.
- The Social Security Act (1935) created a compulsory national system of old-age pensions and a joint federal-state system of unemployment insurance.

The Rural Electrification Administration

In 1935, Roosevelt established the Rural Electrification Administration. At this point less than 20 per cent of farms had electricity. By 1945, electrification of farms had risen to 90 per cent.

Progress?

Standards of living of most Americans began to rise. Again, they had money to spend on consumer goods, leisure and entertainment.

Nevertheless, many continued to live in desperate poverty.

- In the mid-1930s, drought, over-planting and over-grazing combined to create a huge dust bowl in Oklahoma, Arkansas and neighbouring states. Tens of thousands of farm families piled their belongings into ramshackle cars and headed west for California to become migrant labourers.
- In his second inaugural address in 1937, Roosevelt drew attention to 'one third of a nation ill-housed, ill-clad, ill-nourished'.

Establish criteria

Below is a sample exam-style question which requires you to make a judgement. The key term in the question has been underlined. Defining the meaning of the key term can help you establish criteria that you can use to make a judgement.

Read the question, define the key term and then set out two or three criteria based on the key term, which you can use to reach and justify a judgement.

How accurate is it to say that the <u>standard of living</u> of most Americans did not rise in the years 1929–41?

Definition:

_____

_____

Criteria to judge the extent to which standards of living failed to rise between 1929–41:

_____

_____

_____

_____

Reach a judgement

Having defined the key term and established a series of criteria, you should now make a judgement. Consider to what extent the standard of living of Americans rose, fell or stayed the same between 1929 and 1941 according to each criterion. Summarise your judgements below:

Criterion 1:

_____

Criterion 2:

_____

Criterion 3:

_____

Criterion 4:

_____

Finally, sum up your judgement. Based on the criteria, how accurate is it to say that the standard of living of most Americans did not rise in the years 1929–41?

_____

_____

_____

_____

The impact of the Second World War and the growth of a consumer society, 1941–60

The Second World War

Most Americans prospered during the Second World War. The basic economic problem was no longer finding jobs but finding workers for the booming shipyards and aircraft factories. Millions of people, who had lived on the margin in the 1930s, were brought fully into the economic system. Poverty did not disappear, particularly among black families in the South, but for most Americans the war saw increased prosperity.

The main problem for Americans was not lack of money but lack of goods to spend their money on. Many consumer items – cars, washing machines and houses – ceased to be made/built. Another problem was rationing. In 1942, the government introduced the General Maximum Price Regulation, which froze prices. With prices frozen, some goods were allocated through rationing. Rationed goods included sugar, coffee, petrol, meat and car tyres.

A consumer society

For many Americans after 1945, the American dream was a reality. The booming economy led to a sharp rise in **consumerism**. The typical family bought consumer goods that made the US lifestyle envied by many across the world.

New housing

Americans had the money to purchase new houses in suburbia. Suburban growth owed much to the phenomenon of **'white flight'** as white Americans sought to escape cities with high taxes, crowded accommodation, crime and growing ghettos. The most famous builders were the Levitt brothers, who began construction of their first Levittown in Hempstead, Long Island, in 1947. Built primarily for young veterans, Hempstead had 17,000 homes, 80,000 residents, seven shopping centres, nine swimming pools and two bowling alleys. Residents were expected to conform to rules stipulating weekly lawn mowing, no fences and no washing hung out at weekends. Priced at around $8,000, only two and a half times the average family income, Levitt houses were well constructed with central heating, modern bathrooms and kitchens, on building plots twice the normal size. Levittowns soon sprang up all over the USA.

Car ownership

By the 1950s, most American families could afford to buy a car – indeed cars. Cars – long, multi-coloured and decorated with large quantities of chrome – reflected American affluence and self-confidence. Growing car ownership changed lifestyles in the 1950s, making lives easier and more varied. Americans could get to places faster and more comfortably.

The impact of the 'consumer society'

For most Americans, the USA was a land of plenty in the 1950s. Ever-increasing purchasing power enabled Americans not only to buy new houses and cars, but also a variety of labour-saving devices. Washing machines, freezers and dishwashers made housewives' lives easier. Americans could afford television sets, record players and holidays. Advertisements, particularly those on television, encouraged Americans to buy new products of every kind.

Some intellectuals hated the impact of the consumer culture on society:

- Economist John Kenneth Galbraith's *The Affluent Society* (1958) argued that Americans were grossly materialistic and cared little about the less fortunate.

- Others claimed that consumerism and materialism were becoming central to the nation's identity and undermining traditional American values such as hard work and careful money management.

- Some claimed that the consumer society contributed to the standardisation and conformity that characterised suburbia, where everyone had to keep up with their neighbours and have all the latest gadgets and the new car.

- Many intellectuals blamed increasing consumerism and conformity on television and advertisements.

Develop the detail   a

Below are a sample exam question and a paragraph written in answer to this question. The paragraph contains a limited amount of detail. Annotate the paragraph to add additional detail to the answer.

> How far did increasing prosperity have a beneficial effect on American society in the years 1941–60?

> The USA was a land of plenty for many in the 1950s. This economic prosperity encouraged the development of a consumer society that generated social and cultural change. The impact of the car was one example. America became a car-based society.

Developing an argument

Below is a sample exam-style question, a list of key points to be made in the essay and a paragraph from the essay. Read the question, the plan and the sample paragraph. Rewrite the paragraph in order to develop an argument. Your paragraph should explain why the factor discussed in the paragraph is linked to the question. Crucially, it should develop an argument by setting out a general answer to the question and reasons that support this.

> To what extent had Americans never had it so good in the years 1945–60?

Key points

- Prosperity post-1945.
- Affluence and consumerism.
- The benefits of consumerism.
- The critics of consumerism.

> Some intellectuals hated the effect of the consumer culture on American society. Harvard University economist John K. Galbraith claimed in *The Affluent Society* (1958) that his fellow Americans were grossly materialistic and cared little about the less fortunate in society. Sociologist David Riesman argued that consumerism and materialism had become central to the USA's identity and feared that this was undermining 'traditional American values', not least hard work and careful management of money. Historian and sociologist Lewis Mumford believed the consumer society contributed to the standardisation and conformity that characterised suburbia. In suburbia, everyone had to keep up with their neighbours and have a new car and all the latest household gadgets.

The impact of anti-poverty policies and economic divisions, 1961–80

The War on Poverty: Johnson's Great Society

In 1964, Johnson persuaded Congress to pass the Economic Opportunity Act, which provided aid to poor families. This was central to his Great Society vision whereby the federal government would ensure the end of poverty and urban decay and bring about racial equality and educational reform.

The elderly constituted a large proportion of America's poor, partly because of the cost of health care. In 1965, Congress established Medicare and Medicaid.

- Medicare provided federally funded health insurance for over-65s and those with disabilities.
- Medicaid was a scheme whereby federal money was given to states to help them provide essential medical services to those in need.

The situation by 1968

By 1968, it was apparent that the USA could not afford both the Great Society and the Vietnam War. Conservatives bemoaned the fact that too much money was being spent on welfare programmes, which simply increased the poor's dependency on the state. Liberals bemoaned the lack of money spent on Great Society schemes. For many poor, elderly, sick and unemployed, Johnson's schemes did make a difference. But they did not stop the city riots in 1968.

The end of the post-war boom, 1969–80

After 1969, the economic boom faltered.

Nixon's problems

In 1969, Nixon inherited a massive federal deficit, inflation at 4.7 per cent, declining industrial productivity and balance of trade problems:
- Efforts to halt inflation by cutting federal spending failed.
- Nixon's New Economic Policy (1971) introduced the USA's first peacetime wage-price freeze and **devalued** the dollar. The devaluation, which made US exports cheaper, was designed to help the balance of trade. But the USA's economic woes continued.
- A further devaluation of the dollar in 1973 proved equally ineffective.
- When Nixon abandoned wage and price controls in 1973, prices rocketed.

The problem of oil

By 1970, the USA imported a third of its oil, mostly from the Middle East. The oil embargo, resulting from the 1973 **Arab-Israeli War**, revealed America's economic vulnerability. The embargo's end was followed by a near four-fold increase in oil prices. This had a massive impact on the US economy.

Ford and Carter's problems

US economic problems continued under Ford and Carter. In 1973–80 the USA experienced unprecedented inflation (mainly due to rising oil prices and government overspending) which was in or near double figures. As the cost of living rose at a yearly average of 8.2 per cent, this affected family incomes. The hardest hit were those in areas of declining manufacturing output. Increasing numbers of people previously used to well-paid work found themselves unemployed. This was mainly due to:
- increased mechanisation
- countries (like Japan) producing goods at lower prices and often higher quality.

A new energy crisis

The rising cost of energy (especially oil) had damaging consequences.

- In the harsh winter of 1976–77, a gas shortage led to closure of schools and factories in eastern America. Petrol stations cut their hours in order to conserve supplies.
- In 1979, half the USA's petrol stations were without fuel. Those that had it charged 50 per cent more than in 1978. Drivers again had to queue for petrol.
- The inability of Ford, Carter and Congress to solve the fuel crisis and **stagflation** (high inflation and unemployment) contributed to growing political disillusion and the feeling that the USA was in decline.

! Simple essay style

Below is a sample question. Use your own knowledge and the information on the opposite page to produce a plan for this question. Choose four general points and provide three pieces of specific information to support each general point. Once you have planned your essay, write the introduction and conclusion for the essay. The introduction should list the points to be discussed in the essay. The conclusion should summarise the key points and justify which point was the most important.

How accurate is it to say that most Americans experienced a fall in living standards in the years 1960–80?

i Developing an argument

Below is a sample exam-style question, a list of key points to be made in the essay and a paragraph from the essay. Read the question, the plan and the sample paragraph. Rewrite the paragraph in order to develop an argument. Your paragraph should explain why the factor discussed in the paragraph is linked to the question. Crucially, it should develop an argument by setting out a general answer to the question and reasons that support this.

To what extent was the high cost of oil to blame for the USA's growing economic problems in the years 1969–80?

Key points

- Economic problems in 1969.
- Nixon's policies.
- The 1973 oil crisis.
- Rising inflation.
- Rising unemployment.
- The continuing fuel crisis.

Cheap oil had been vital to the USA's post-1945 boom. However, by 1970 nearly a third of the USA's oil was imported, mostly from the Middle East. The USA's dependency on Middle East oil became apparent in 1973 when the Arab–Israeli War led to an oil embargo on the USA. The end of the embargo was followed by a steep rise in the price of oil. The end of the era of cheap energy hit Americans' standard of living. Increased oil prices also contributed to inflation.

The reasons for, and the impact of, increased leisure time, 1917–80

1917–30

Growing prosperity and reductions in work hours after 1919 resulted in Americans having the means to enjoy leisure pursuits. In the 1920s, Americans embraced commercial entertainment as never before. In 1919, they spent £2.5 billion on leisure activities. By 1929, spending on leisure was $4.3 billion, a figure not equalled until after the Second World War. Spectator amusements – Hollywood films, music and sports – accounted for a fifth of the 1929 total. The rest involved participatory recreation, such as games, hobbies and travel.

- Entrepreneurs responded quickly to an appetite for fads. In the early 1920s, mahjong, a Chinese tile game, was the craze. In the mid-1920s, crossword puzzles, printed in mass-circulation newspapers and magazines, were popular. By 1930, miniature golf had become the new fad.
- The spread of automobiles (see page 82), paved highways and tourist cabins stimulated tourism to national parks, beaches and big cities.
- Church attendance and events associated with the Church involved millions.
- When staying at home, Americans listened to radio, and devoured mass magazines such as *Reader's Digest*.

Prohibition

One leisure activity that Americans could not enjoy (legally) in the 1920s was having an alcoholic drink, whether at home or in a pub or restaurant. The 18th Amendment, which prohibited the sale, manufacture or transport of alcoholic beverages, came into force in 1920. It was supported by the Volstead Act (1919). Thousands of illicit stills were seized, millions of gallons of wine and spirits were destroyed and prison sentences for liquor offences rose to 45,000 in 1932. In small towns and rural areas, the law was generally observed and there was a marked drop in alcoholism. However, a sizeable minority of Americans, including the rich and the immigrant working class, regarded Prohibition as an infringement of personal liberty and simply defied it. 'Bootleggers' smuggled in liquor from the West Indies, Mexico and Canada while domestic distillers illicitly manufactured 'moonshine' and 'mountain dew'. Obliging doctors supplied liquor prescriptions to chronic sufferers from 'thirstitis'. 'Speakeasies' (illicit saloons) and night clubs flourished. In 1929, there were 32,000 speakeasies in New York City – twice the number of saloons before Prohibition began. Prohibition finally came to an end in 1933 – although some states remained 'dry'.

Leisure restrictions, 1930–45

The coming of the Depression and then the impact of the Second World War meant that some Americans had less money – and time – to spend on commercial leisure activities. However, the majority of people continued to pursue similar activities to those they had enjoyed during the prosperous 1920s – going to the movies, listening to the radio, watching (and playing) sport – as well as pursuing hobbies like walking, gardening, fishing, reading and sewing.

1945–80

Commercialised leisure, increasingly controlled by multinational media conglomerates, expanded its reach. Television viewing, movie-going, the recording industry, sport and the travel industry flourished. The USA's first theme park, Disneyland, opened in 1955, followed by scores of others – including Disney World which opened in Orlando, Florida, in 1971. With the introduction of jet aircraft (see page 82), foreign travel, once an elite activity, became accessible to large numbers of Americans. But most Americans continued to take their holidays in the USA – in places as diverse as Las Vegas, the many national parks and the coastal areas.

Not all leisure was commercialised. Americans continued to enjoy more small-scale diversions, from camping and hiking to reading and gardening. They continued to participate in community- and church-based recreational events, and took part in activities such as bowling and softball. Despite its mass culture aspects, leisure in the USA in the late-twentieth century remained highly diverse and individual.

! Simple essay style

Below is a sample exam question. Use your own knowledge and the information on the opposite page to produce a plan for this question. Choose four general points, and provide three pieces of specific information to support each general point. Once you have planned your essay, write the introduction and conclusion for the essay. The introduction should list the points to be discussed in the essay. The conclusion should summarise the key points and justify which point was the most important.

To what extent were Americans able to enjoy leisure pursuits in the period 1917–45?

⦂ Identify key terms

Below is a sample exam question which includes a key word or term. Key terms are important because their meaning can be helpful in structuring your answer, developing an argument and establishing criteria that will help form the basis of a judgement.

To what extent was American leisure dominated by commercial entertainment in the years 1917–80?

- First, identify the key word or term. This will be a word or phrase that is important to the meaning of the question. Underline the word or phrase.
- Secondly, define the key phrase. Your definition should set out the key features of the phrase or word that you are defining.
- Third, make an essay plan that reflects your definition.
- Finally, write a sentence answering the question that refers back to the definition.

The growth of spectator sports

1917–45

Sport became big business after 1917. Millions of Americans packed stadiums to watch sporting events. Most sports were racially segregated. Black sportsmen, banned from playing in the major white leagues, formed their own leagues.

Baseball

Baseball was the most popular spectator sport. It survived the scandal arising from members of the Chicago White Sox revealing that they had accepted bribes to throw the 1919 World Series. 'Babe' Ruth's ability to hit home runs for the New York Yankees helped to repair baseball's image. (He hit 60 in 1927 – a record.) Discovering that home runs excited fans, the leagues redesigned the ball to make it livelier. Game attendance skyrocketed. A record 300,000 people attended the six-game 1921 World Series between the New York Giants and New York Yankees. Millions gathered to watch local teams and even more listened to professional games on the radio. (Ronald Reagan made his reputation initially as a baseball commentator.)

Boxing

In 1920, boxing was legalised in New York, which then became the recognised centre of the sport. World title fights attracted huge crowds. Jack Dempsey, the world heavyweight champion in 1919–26, attracted gates in excess of a million dollars. His 1927 rematch with Gene Tunney, the man who dethroned him, attracted a crowd of over 100,000.

American football

College and professional American football both grew in popularity.

College football

- Large-scale stadia were built at many universities/colleges. In 1928, the University of Michigan built a stadium seating 87,000 people.
- 'Red' Grange, the 'Galloping Ghost', was a major star of the University of Illinois.
- The most famous coach was Knute Rockne. During his 13 years as coach at Notre Dame (1918–31), his teams won 105 games, lost 12 and tied 15.

Professional football

In 1920, the American Professional Association – soon renamed the National Football League (NFL) – was organised. It was primarily a Midwestern organisation of company-sponsored squads. Initially, the NFL had a hard time competing with College football for fan support. Public support grew when 'Red' Grange signed for the Chicago Bears in 1925.

1945–80

Spectators attended sporting events in massive numbers. Even more watched on television. American football and baseball remained the most popular sports but basketball and ice hockey also attracted large audiences – as did boxing, tennis, golf and horse racing. By the late 1950s, sports were no longer segregated. Indeed, by the 1970s many – if not most – of the main 'stars' were black. As cities competed to gain or protect sports teams that symbolised urban prestige, professional franchises became lucrative. Buttressed by enthusiastic fans (increasingly women as well as men), powerful economic interests and saturation television coverage, professional sports occupied a secure niche in popular culture by 1980.

American football

After 1945, professional American football became more popular than baseball, partly because it was more exciting on television.

- The establishment of the American Football League in 1960 encouraged the NFL to expand.
- A bidding war for players led to a merger of the leagues in 1966.
- The first Super Bowl took place in 1967.

Baseball

- In 1947, Branch Rickey, coach of the Brooklyn Dodgers, signed Jackie Robinson – the first black major leaguer. By 1960, every major league club had black players.
- In the 1950s, the Brooklyn Dodgers and New York Giants moved to California, essentially for financial reasons.
- In the 1970s, clubs discovered a new source of talent in Latin American players.

Support or challenge?

Below is a sample exam-style question which asks you to what extent you agree with a specific statement. Below that is a list of general statements which are relevant to the question. Using your own knowledge and the information on the opposite page, decide whether these statements support or challenge the statement in question.

How far do you agree that radio and television had a crucial effect on the popularity of American spectator sports in the years 1917–80?

STATEMENT	SUPPORT	CHALLENGE
Sporting events attracted huge crowds before radio broadcasts.		
Millions of Americans listened to baseball commentaries on the radio in the 1920s and 30s.		
Millions of Americans watched local teams play baseball and college football in the 1920s and 30s.		
Radio enhanced interest in sport in the 1920s and 1930s.		
Television helped popularise professional American football after 1950.		
Huge television coverage led to a fall in sporting attendances.		
The Super Bowl became an enormous television spectacle.		
By the 1970s there was huge coverage of all major sporting events on American television channels.		

Spectrum of importance

Below are a sample exam question and a list of general points which could be used to answer the question. Use your own knowledge and the information on the opposite page to reach a judgement about the importance of these general points to the question posed. Write numbers on the spectrum below to indicate their relative importance. Having done this, write a brief justification of your placement, explaining why some of these factors are more important than others. The resulting diagram could form the basis of an essay plan.

How accurate is to say that baseball was the most popular American spectator sport in the years 1917–80?

1 Baseball attendances

2 The influence of Babe Ruth

3 Radio and television coverage of baseball

4 The popularity of American football

5 The popularity of other sports

Least important ←——————————————→ Most important

Car-owning and improved air travel, post-1945

REVISED

Car ownership

By 1960, 80 per cent of American families owned at least one car and 14 per cent had two or more. Nearly all were manufactured in the USA. Most were designed to go out of fashion within a year or two, promoting further purchases. Spacious new cars with automatic transmission, radios, heaters and air conditioning provided a pleasant means of travel. Petrol prices were low, so driving was cheap.

The impact of the car on American life

Growing car ownership changed American lifestyles in the 1950s.

- Americans who lived in the suburbs were totally dependent on automobiles.
- Cars enabled Americans to tour their country.
- Americans could watch films and even attend church from the comfort of their cars.

The car symbolised the identification of freedom with individual choice and mobility. Americans could imagine themselves as modern versions of western pioneers, able to leave behind urban crowds for the 'open road.' The 'open road' was not 'open' for long. Large areas of rural America became covered by roads and adjacent motels, restaurants, stores, parking lots and advertisements.

Air travel

The 1950s

The US air transport industry underwent rapid expansion. This reflected:
- the nation's economic growth.
- aircraft development. By the early 1950s Douglas DC-6s and Lockheed Constellations could carry more than 50 passengers from New York to California in ten hours.

More than 38 million passengers used American domestic airlines in 1955 – the first year that airlines carried more people than railways. By 1958, international airlines took more travellers to Europe than steamship companies.

The 1960s

With the introduction of jet aircraft, foreign travel became accessible to more Americans. But most used planes to travel within the USA. Reduction in airline fares lured travellers away from trains and buses. By the mid-1960s, 50 per cent of airline passengers were travelling for pleasure rather than business. The number of passengers carried by scheduled airlines rose from 56.3 million in 1960 to 158.5 million in 1969. The 1960s was a golden age for the air-transport industry. The major companies grew larger, regional airlines prospered and scheduled air flights brought air service to small communities.

The 1970s and 80s

The good times ended in the 1970s.

- The appearance of 'jumbo jets' (for example, the Boeing 747) added capacity at a time when demand was levelling off.
- The oil crisis of 1973–74 (see page 76) quadrupled airline fuel prices.
- The economic 'stagflation' of the later 1970s further depressed the airline industry.
- The Airline Deregulation Act (1978) ended the government's control over routes and fares. Airlines were now free to add or drop routes as market conditions dictated and to charge whatever fares they pleased. New airlines proliferated in the unregulated environment, increasing from 36 in 1978 to 96 in 1983.
- The Professional Air Traffic Controllers Organisation began an illegal strike in 1981, crippling the air traffic system. President Reagan fired 11,000 strikers, breaking both the strike and the union. But several years elapsed before air traffic control fully recovered.
- Between 1979–83, the domestic airline industry suffered a net loss of $1.2 billion.
- The late 1980s witnessed a wave of mergers and bankruptcies.

Despite these problems, Americans continued to fly. By the 1980s, air travel had changed from an individual adventure to a routine feature of American life.

! Mind map artwork

Use the information on the opposite page and your own knowledge to add detail (at least two points) to the mind map below.

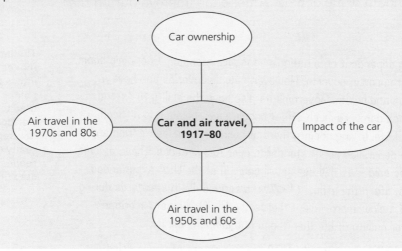

! Spot the mistake   a

Below are a sample exam question and a paragraph written in answer to this question. Why does this paragraph not get into Level 4? Once you have identified the mistake, rewrite the paragraph so that it displays the qualities of Level 4. The mark scheme on pages 109–10 will help you.

How accurate is it to say that the automobile dominated American leisure activities in the years 1945–80?

The automobile industry employed tens of thousands of Americans. Most of the cars on American roads by the 1950s were manufactured in Detroit by General Motors, Ford and Chrysler. Their products — long, multi-coloured and decorated with large quantities of chrome — reflected the USA's affluence and self-confidence. Automobile manufacturers and advertisers tried to persuade Americans to buy new cars as often as possible. Consumers, anxious to keep up with their neighbours, obliged. Some 4.5 million cars were scrapped each year in the 1950s. The increased mobility that cars offered contributed to the dramatic growth of the service industries and the changing nature of the American workforce.

Exam focus

Below is a sample essay. Read it and the comments around it.

To what extent did the standard of life of most Americans improve during the years 1921–41?

Standards of life are essentially dependent on a nation's economic standing. Economic boom usually results in affluence, depression in poverty. However, new discoveries can have a major impact on leisure activities and health. Governments also have the ability to extend or restrict people's freedom which can very much affect people's well-being. It is difficult to generalise about standards of life. In any society there are winners and losers, rich and poor. It is even more difficult to generalise about standards over two decades. These axioms out of the way, it can broadly be said – as this essay will say – that the USA experienced improvements in the standard of life in the affluent 1920s, a serious dip in standards during the Depression (1929–33) and a slow improvement thereafter. By 1941 most Americans almost certainly enjoyed a better quality of life than those two decades earlier.

Once the brief depression of 1919–21 was over, the USA entered an era of unparalleled prosperity. Businesses made huge profits and there was little unemployment. Americans worked less, produced more, were paid more and were healthier than ever before. Standards of living thus rose. This was reflected in the fact that Americans were able to buy a variety of new electrical household appliances – cookers, irons and fridges – which took away some of the drudgery of housework. Many Americans were even able to afford new houses in which to put the new gadgets. Thanks to Henry Ford, cars also became affordable. By 1929 there were nearly 27 million cars – one car for every five Americans. Cars meant greater mobility and freedom. People had the time and money to go to the cinema, to take a holiday and to attend sporting events. By 1930, nearly half of all American homes possessed a radio. In the 1928 election, presidential candidate Herbert Hoover was able to promise Americans 'a chicken in every pot and two cars in every garage'. 'We shall soon with the help of God', he said, 'be in sight of the day when poverty will be banished from this nation.'

However, not all Americans were prosperous in the Roaring Twenties. Coal miners and textile workers did not see their wages rise. Farmers also suffered as a decline in foreign demand and the withdrawal of government price supports after 1920 led to a drastic fall in farm prices. Black families, both in the northern cities and in the South, were America's poorest citizens. They suffered from segregation and discrimination, particularly in the South where their freedoms were restricted. All Americans had their freedoms restricted by the introduction of Prohibition in 1919. Prohibition was part of a wider movement to enforce moral conformity by law. Some states outlawed gambling, made petting a crime (along with extra-marital intercourse) and forbade the sale of contraceptive devices. There was strict local censorship of books, plays and films. Curtailment of freedom had a negative impact on the quality, if not the standard, of life in the 1920s.

The Great Depression, which followed the Wall Street Crash in 1929, had a catastrophic effect on most Americans' standard of life. By mid-1932, industrial output had dropped to half the 1929 level and by December 1932 unemployment was over 12 million – a quarter of the work force. There was no dole. Thus, unemployment brought real fear and despair. Millions of people roamed the countryside, stealing rides on freight trains and looking for work. Others congregated on the outskirts of cities in shanty towns known as Hoovervilles. It was not just the unemployed who suffered. Those lucky enough to be in full-time work saw their average earnings fall by a third. Many were only employed part time. Farmers, badly off to begin with, suffered more than anyone as farm prices collapsed. The Depression thus

The introduction makes some interesting points but does tend to ramble. Nor do the first few sentences really engage the reader – or the question.

This is a good paragraph, displaying excellent knowledge and understanding. The final two quotes are impressive and relevant.

The first few sentences need to be said. Whether the last few sentences are fully relevant is a moot point. In fairness, the candidate accepts this with the 'quality' of life comment.

A strong paragraph which is well written and relevant to the set question.

Quick quizzes at **www.hoddereducation.co.uk/myrevisionnotes**

had a draconian effect on the standard of lives of Americans, particularly blacks. In northern cities, they were usually the first to be fired. In the South, where 75 per cent still lived, many were dependent upon cotton, the crop hardest hit by the Depression. Grim though American sufferings were during the Depression, they were not comparable to those of, say, the USSR in 1920–21 when famine claimed millions of lives. The total reported number of deaths from starvation in the early 1930s in America was 110. Even so there was a dramatic rise in cases of malnutrition. As late as 1935, it was estimated that 20 million people were not getting enough to eat.

After 1933, the economic situation began gradually to improve. President Roosevelt accepted that the government had a final responsibility for the well-being of its citizens. His New Deal measures provided work for some Americans while his 1935 Social Security Act created a compulsory national system of old-age pensions and a joint federal–state system of unemployment insurance. It should be said the Act had major defects, not least that no payments could be made until 1942. At best, the New Deal brought about only partial recovery: some 10 million Americans were still out of work in 1939. Nevertheless, it did give the USA new roads, dams, hospitals and sports facilities. The Rural Electrification Administration also brought electrification of farms. Historian Michael Heale claims that probably no other single measure of the New Deal was as responsible as this for transforming life in the South. Perhaps above all else, Roosevelt gave Americans hope. Whether this is a standard of life issue is a moot point – but perhaps in some way it is. Roosevelt also gave most Americans alcohol. The 1933 Congress passed the 21st Amendment, repealing the 18th Amendment. Control over drinking reverted to the states. Only seven of them voted to retain Prohibition.

> This paragraph is a bit thin on detail. Perhaps the candidate is running out of steam or time. The New Deal was worth a bit more attention.

After the outbreak of war in Europe in 1939 the US economy finally began to recover big time as American firms 'stole' European markets and the USA began to make its own preparations for war. By 1941, unemployment was falling fast and most Americans were again enjoying a standard of living that was probably the best in the world. The affluence was to continue until the 1970s.

> This paragraph is even thinner.

By 1941, most Americans enjoyed a much better standard of life than they had enjoyed in 1921. That said, for many it was not much better than that experienced in 1928–29 prior to the Depression. Few Americans in 1941 believed (as Hoover had in 1928) that poverty was about to be eradicated. Nor were they necessarily confident about the future. By 1941, many could see that war was probably coming and few thought this would have a positive impact on the standard of life. In his 1941 State of the Union message, President Roosevelt included 'freedom from want' on his list of the Four Freedoms' (along with speech, religion and freedom from fear). By 1941, Americans had freedom of speech and religion. Most – but not all – had freedom from want. With war in the offing, it is unlikely that all Americans felt freedom from fear.

> The conclusion makes some very relevant points. But the final sentences on Roosevelt's Four Freedoms do not seem particularly relevant. Nor do they pull the essay together. A pity. There is some potential here but it is not fully realised.

This answer is probably just about a Level 4 – on the strength of its contextual knowledge and the fact that it is well written. Its main failing is the fact that it never quite gets to grips with the question. The introduction and conclusion tend to drift off target and are not fully focused.

Moving from a Level 4 to Level 5

The other exam focus essays on pages 26–7, 46–7, and 66–7 provided Level 5 answers. The essay here achieves a Level 4. Read the Level 5 essays and the comments provided. Make a list of the additional features required to push a Level 4 essay into Level 5.

5 Historical interpretations: What impact did the Reagan presidency have on the USA in the years 1981–89?

Ronald Reagan becomes president, 1980–81

REVISED

The 1980 election

The 1980 election pitted Ronald Reagan, a Republican, against Democrat Jimmy Carter.

Ronald Reagan

Reagan was born in Illinois in 1911 to relatively poor parents. Careers in three forms of media – radio in the mid-1930s, movies from the late 1930s to the mid-1950s and television from the mid-1950s to the mid-1960s – gave him unparalleled tuition in the political arts of communication, image-making and performance. Once a fervent supporter of the New Deal, he had moved to the right in the 1950s, becoming the idol of those Republicans who approved of his attacks on big government. In 1966, he became governor of California, appealing to voters who resented high taxes, affirmative action programmes, rising crime and the challenges to traditional values.

Carter's unpopularity

By 1980, most Americans believed their country was drifting.

- There were serious concerns with regard to the energy crisis, economic decline and rising crime.
- Foreign reverses suggested that the USSR was poised to become the world's dominant power.
- The Iranian hostage crisis, which TV reported on daily, reminded viewers of Carter's apparent weakness.

The Religious Right

Many Americans – the so-called New Right or Religious Right – were hostile to liberal reforms and the permissive society associated with the Democrats. In 1979, Jerry Falwell, a Virginia minister, established Moral Majority. It claimed that supporters of abortion, easy divorce and military unpreparedness were agents of the Devil. Reagan could count on the Religious Right's support. The Republican platform condemned moral permissiveness and supported 'family values'.

Reagan's problems

- Democrats tried to make Reagan's right-wing views and his age (he was 69) central issues in the campaign.
- Reagan faced opposition from a third candidate, John Anderson, a moderate conservative, who stood for the newly formed National Unity Party.

The final TV debate

Reagan and Carter remained even in the polls until the final TV debate on 28 October, in which Reagan posed the most telling question of the campaign: 'Are you better off than you were four years ago?' Most political commentators thought Reagan won the debate convincingly. So did most voters.

The result

Reagan won a bare majority (50.7 per cent) of the popular vote but that was well ahead of Carter's 41 per cent. In the Electoral College, Reagan's victory was overwhelming – 489 to 44. The Republicans won control of the Senate for the first time in 25 years. They also gained seats in the House of Representatives but the Democrats remained in control there.

Inauguration

Reagan's installation was a triumph of showbiz spectacle. In his inaugural address, Reagan promised a 'new beginning'. The tax system, 'which penalises successful achievement and keeps us from maintaining full productivity', was the central point of attack.

Assassination attempt

In March 1981, Reagan was shot and severely wounded. His bravery/humour – 'Honey, I forgot to duck' he told his wife, Nancy – endeared him to most Americans. A number of Congressional Democrats, impressed by his popularity and recovery, were prepared to support some of his measures.

RAG – rate the extract

Below are a sample Section C exam question and one of the extracts referred to in the question. Read the question, study the extract and, using three coloured pens, underline it in red, amber or green to show:

Red: the interpretation offered by the extract

Amber: evidence that supports this interpretation

Green: counter-arguments and counter-evidence provided by the extract

> In the light of differing interpretations, how convincing do you find the view that Ronald Reagan came to power in 1981 with a clear, rational and well-thought through programme which he had every intention of implementing?

EXTRACT 1

From Bill Boyarsky, Ronald Reagan: His Life and Rise to the Presidency, *published in 1981.*

As President, Reagan quickly moved beyond the words of that patriotic, simplistic [inaugural] address. As he had promised in his speeches, and as he had done in California, he sought to change the direction of government. He filled his Administration with like-minded men. The conservative quality of his assistants was assured by the informal 'kitchen cabinet' which supervised major appointments. ... Adopting the policies of conservative economic advisers, Reagan immediately proposed an income tax cut that was designed to revive the economy by increasing spendable private income. He proposed discarding or limiting social programmes he considered failures. In short, he turned the nation onto a new course, one much more sympathetic to the corporations that control much of American life. With his words Reagan intended to revive the national spirit, and with his policies he would let the corporations revive the economy. There were hard times ahead. Special-interest groups protested an Administration that so clearly wanted to change the nation's direction. In one of those terrible events that too often determine the course of history, a young man shot him. But Reagan survived the attempted assassination with remarkable strength, humour and luck, and went on to the difficult and complex job he faced.

The effect of Reagan's economic policies

Reaganomics

Reagan hoped to solve the problem of 'stagflation'.

Reagan's aims

In the 1980 campaign, Reagan had proposed to cut taxes and domestic spending but increase military spending. He claimed he would be able to reduce the **budget deficit** with the increased revenues that would pour in from a rejuvenated economy. He also wished to see far less government interference in economic matters. His 'supply-side' economics (dubbed 'trickle-down' economics or 'Reaganomics' by critics) derived from a group of economists who challenged the Keynesian doctrine that the problems of the economy were mainly on the demand side. Supply-siders claimed that economic problems resulted from government intrusion into the marketplace and from excessive taxes that hampered incentives to work, save and invest. They favoured high interest rates to curb inflation.

Reaganomics in action

- The Economic Recovery Tax Act (1981) decreased taxes. This mainly benefited the wealthy.
- In 1981, the administration recommended budget cuts of $35.2 billion. These were aimed mainly at welfare programmes.
- Reagan promised to retain the 'safety net' for the 'truly needy'. Rather than encourage welfare recipients to seek work, his new approach was to provide aid only for those who could not work because of disability or child care. The result was that welfare spending was hardly reduced.
- Given the increase in defence spending, Reagan's administration increased expenditure, thereby massively increasing the national debt.

Problems in 1981–82

In 1982, the government deficit nearly doubled to $110.6 billion and the total national debt went above $1 trillion. Reagan's response was the Tax Equity and Fiscal Responsibility Bill (1982), which reversed some of the 1981 tax concessions to business and increased taxes on cigarettes and airline tickets. The USA suffered a severe recession as many Americans lost their jobs. 'Stay the course' was Reagan's slogan. Perseverance would give the tax cuts time to work their magic.

Success?

By 1983, Reagan's measures seemed to be having some success

- A decline in world oil prices led to inflation falling below 2 per cent.
- Unemployment began to fall. Many new jobs were created by Reagan's increase in defence spending (c.$1.5 trillion between 1981 and 1984).

Tax reform

In 1986, Congress supported Reagan's proposal for tax simplification by passing a comprehensive Tax Reform Act – the first major revamping of the federal income tax system for 40 years. This:

- reduced the number of tax brackets from 14 to two
- reduced tax rates – the highest tax rate went down from 50 per cent to 28 per cent
- exempted millions of low-income families from tax payment.

The situation by 1989

In the period 1983–89, the USA created 18 million new jobs. There was far less unemployment. There was no longer an inflation problem. These were huge achievements.

However, there was a down side.

- During the Reagan years there were mounting deficits in the balance of trade which weakened the dollar and turned the USA into a debtor nation for the first time since 1914.
- By 1986, the National Debt had doubled from $1 trillion to $2 trillion. Paying interest on the debt became the third largest item in the federal budget.

Ironically, it is hard for the left to be too critical of Reagan's economic policies or the right to be too positive. Arguably, by spending so much on defence, he carried out **Keynesian economics**, creating jobs and not worrying too much about the consequences. Perhaps there was no need to worry. Liberal economists' predictions that the enormous national debt would have catastrophic effects on America's future turned out to be wide of the mark.

Summarise the interpretations

Below are a sample Section C exam question and the two accompanying extracts. The extracts offer different interpretations of the issue raised by the question. After reading each extract summarise the interpretation it offers.

Extract 1 argues

_____

_____

Extract 2 argues

_____

_____

> In the light of differing interpretations how convincing do you find the view that President Reagan dealt very successfully with the economic problems he faced in 1981? (Extract 2)

_____

_____

Historians have different views about the success of Reagan's economic policies. Analyse and evaluate the extracts and use your knowledge of the issues to explain your answer to the following question. How far do you agree with the view that President Reagan dealt ineffectively with the economic problems he faced in 1981?

EXTRACT 1

From William H. Chafe, The Unfinished Journey: America Since World War II, _published in 1999_

The world's largest creditor nation in 1980, America now became the world's largest debtor nation, with a trade imbalance that soared to $170 billion by 1987. It was all a vicious spiral downward, fueled by indebtedness. The interest on national debt alone took as much money as it cost to run nine departments of government, including Labour, Commerce, Education and Agriculture; and the more the budget and trade deficits grew, the harder it would be for the American economy to reclaim its independence and self-sufficiency. It required the output of 1.5 million American workers simply to pay America's interest on the debt it owed to the rest of the world. In the face of such realities, one economist concluded 'the potential for disaster is very great'. Even more disturbing were some of the deeper structural changes that flowed from these realities. More and more American workers, for example, were forced to seek employment in low-wage service industries. Although more new jobs were created in the 1980s than were lost, half of those that were lost were in relatively high-paying industries; on the other hand half of the new jobs paid wages below the poverty level for a family of four. Hence, the number of low wage earners increased substantially during the 1980s at the expense of high wage jobs that either disappeared or moved overseas.

EXTRACT 2

From Martin Anderson, Revolution, _published in 1988_

It was the greatest economic expansion in history. Wealth poured from the factories of the United States, and Americans got richer and richer. During the five years between November 1982 and November 1987 more wealth and services were produced than in any like period in history. There were 60 straight months of uninterrupted economic growth, the longest string of steady peacetime growth in national production since we first began to keep such statistics in 1854. Close to fifteen million new jobs were created. It was the greatest five-year employment growth in U.S. history. At the end of 1982 the number of Americans working was 100,697,000. Five years later 115,494,000 were working. The production of wealth in the United States was stupendous. Reagan's run from the end of 1982 to the end of 1987 produced just a hair under $20 trillion dollars of goods and services, measured in actual dollars, unadjusted for inflation or changes in the quality of goods and services. The sum is so large that the value of the treasure is perhaps beyond comprehension ... By the end of 1987 the United States was producing about seven and a half times more every year than it produced the last year John F. Kennedy was president. By then we were producing 65 percent a year more than when Jimmy Carter left office in January 1981.

The extent to which big government was reduced

Reagan's intent

Reagan had long stated his opposition to big government. 'Government is not the solution to our problems: government is the problem', he declared. He was determined to free the government from control by 'special interests' – by which he meant racial minorities, union leaders and others who wished to attack social inequalities. Consequently, under Reagan the federal government abdicated some of its responsibilities.

Regulation

Reagan was critical of the power and activities of federal regulatory agencies. He believed they were costly, heavy-handed and stifled initiatives. He appointed as heads of these agencies people who shared his conservative view. Consequently there was a reduction in regulation. This policy of deregulation affected agencies like the Consumer Product Safety Commission and the Environmental Protection Agency.

Energy

Reagan believed the federal government should decrease its participation in the field of energy. In 1981, he announced his desire to dismantle the Department of Energy. To help alleviate the energy crisis, Reagan (by executive degree) removed the federal government's regulations on the price of domestic oil and natural gas, thus permitting a rise in the cost of both. His purpose was twofold:

● to reduce consumption
● to stimulate the search for additional energy sources by American oil and gas companies.

Little effort was made to make the USA less dependent on petroleum through conservation or making use of alternative energy sources.

Environmentalism

Reagan had little interest in 'green' issues.

● He took an anti-environmentalist position on the use of land for industrial purposes.
● Little was done to regulate the nuclear industry, which was responsible for some serious leaks from military complexes.

Social issues

Reagan's administration tried to shift the remaining social welfare programmes from the federal government to state and local governments.

Reagan's style

Reagan gave the impression of being the opposite of a workaholic. One reporter wrote: 'He rose at the crack of noon'. He enjoyed vacations at his California ranch and distanced himself from many day-to-day crises. He was content to outline broad policy themes and leave the implementation to others. His cabinet, composed for the most part of able conservatives, had considerable freedom. But Reagan was far from a political novice. After all, he had been governor of California in the turbulent 1960s.

Reagan in action

Reagan was prepared to use his presidential powers when he thought it important to do so.

Organised labour

In 1981, 12,000 air-traffic controllers, members of the Professional Air Traffic Controllers Union, violating a no-strike agreement, struck for higher wages and shorter hours. Reagan fired the workers, sent in the military and revoked the federal government's certification of the Union. He directed the Department of Transportation to train 12,000 people to fill the vacant air traffic control posts. By breaking the strike in this way, he intimidated the labour movement and enhanced his own decisive image.

Foreign Policy

Reagan played an important role in foreign affairs. Determined to stand firm against the USSR, his administration supported anti-Communist movements across the world. However, after 1985 he established a cordial relationship with Soviet leader Gorbachev. This helped bring about a Nuclear Forces treaty in 1987 – the first accord for comprehensive nuclear arms control.

Defence

'Defence is not a budget item', Reagan declared. 'You spend what you need'. Huge sums were spent on a variety of weapons. Reagan was particularly fascinated by the notion of a space shield that would protect the USA from Soviet missiles. Research into the viability of this idea was undertaken. This concerned Soviet leaders, who were aware that the USSR lacked the technology and money to compete with the USA.

Conclusion

In general, the USA under Reagan saw less interference by the government in domestic matters (as he had promised) but more interference on the world stage.

Contrasting interpretations

Below are a sample Section C question and the accompanying extracts. The extracts offer different interpretations of the issue raised by the question. Identify the interpretation offered in each extract and complete the table below, indicating how far the extracts agree with each other and explaining your answer.

	Extent of agreement	Justification
Extracts 1 and 2		

> In the light of differing interpretations, how convincing do you find the view that Ronald Reagan's presidency saw a significant decline in the role of big government? (Extract 2)

Study Extracts 1 and 2. Historians have different views about the extent to which President Reagan reduced the role of the federal government in the USA. Analyse and evaluate the extracts and use your knowledge of the issue to explain your answer to the following question. To what extent did President Reagan reduce the role of the federal government in the USA in the years 1981–89?

EXTRACT 1

From Martin Anderson, Revolution, *published in 1988*

The Reagan administration gets a lot of credit for increasing national defence spending but, somehow, what happened in the huge area of spending for social security, medicare and health seems to have been neglected, benignly. In 1980 we spent $40 billion a year more on these programmes than on national defence. After seven years of Reagan, after the largest military spending streak of any country in history, the United States is still spending $37 billion a year more on social security, medicare and health programmes than it is on national defence.

The programme receiving the next biggest spending increase under Reagan was welfare. Spending on the poor was just over $86 billion a year in 1980. By 1987 President Reagan had largely done on a national level what he had done as governor of California – tried hard to get people off the welfare rolls who could take care of themselves, and then supported substantial increases in welfare spending. In 1987 federal spending for the poor was up by over $38 billion a year to a total of almost $125 billion a year – a 44 per cent increase under Reagan.

EXTRACT 2

From Maldwyn A. Jones, The Limits of Liberty: American History 1607–1992, *published in 1995*

Reagan had long believed that government regulation of the economy, besides being inefficient, often placed unnecessary burdens on business and restricted consumer choice. As president he promised deregulation in a variety of ways. He appointed a task force on regulatory relief, suspended some existing regulations, relaxed the enforcement of others and halted the growth of regulatory budgets. He also staffed regulatory agencies with people unsympathetic to the idea of governmental control – a glaring example being his first Secretary of the Interior, James Watt, who tried to transfer public lands together with their timber and mineral resources to private ownership. In practice, however, the number of federal regulations continued to grow, though more slowly than before, and significant deregulation was achieved only in banking, oil-drilling, coal-mining and transportation. The White House claimed that deregulation had revitalised these industries, besides saving the government money and reducing paperwork. But critics argued that such benefits, if they had indeed occurred, had been won at the cost of lowering standards of protection in health, road and air safety, and other areas.

The nature and extent of social change

Reagan's aims

Reagan was a social conservative. So were his supporters. The 'New Right' tended to be anti-permissiveness, anti-government regulation, patriotic and strongly religious. Reagan agreed with much of their agenda.

- He believed in traditional values and had little time for new 'isms'.
- He was against excessive government interference and did not think it was the government's job to bring about social change. In 1980–81, he vowed he would 'get the government off our backs'.
- He was patriotic.

He was not particularly religious. Nor did he provide an ideal model for the 'Religious Right'. He was the first divorced president, had something of a dysfunctional family and as a Hollywood star had been very much a playboy.

Reagan's policies

Reagan generally showed little interest in social matters.

Welfare

Reagan's administration conducted something of an assault on the social welfare programmes of the 1960s and 70s. Reagan saw welfare programmes as a disincentive to work, which worsened the plight of the poor. There was thus a sharp reduction in spending on **food stamps**, school meals and childcare. Little help was also given to the increasing number of homeless. However, social security, Medicare and farming subsidy costs actually grew during Reagan's presidency.

Civil rights

Reagan claimed that he was not biased against anyone because of race or religion. He was probably right. He got on with people of every creed and colour. However, being opposed to much of the 1960s and 70s legislation, he did little on the civil rights front.

- He supported the Justice Department in its efforts to undo the various affirmative action programmes that gave job or education preference based on race or gender.
- He opposed the bussing of students to schools in other neighbourhoods.
- His appointments to the Civil Rights Commission were undistinguished.
- In the 1980s, black males fell further than any group in terms of wages and jobs.

Immigration

He did very little to limit immigration. By 1990, the USA had a population of 250 million. There were 31 million blacks, 22 million Hispanics and 7 million Asians.

Abortion

He was an outspoken opponent of abortion and encouraged anti-abortion organisations. He stated his unequivocal hope that the Supreme Court would overturn the 1973 decision which permitted abortion on demand.

Gays

Reagan said very little about gay rights.

- He spent little government money to fund research or help the victims of AIDS in the late 1980s.
- The Supreme Court in *Bowers v Hardwick* (1986) upheld the constitutionality of state laws outlawing homosexual acts.

Law and order

He favoured a tough stance on law and order. He was particularly opposed to drug abuse. Some 750,000 Americans faced drug charges each year in the 1980s. Most were prosecuted for smoking marijuana. But **crack** became a real problem in the 1980s. By 1988, $15 billion was spent by government authorities in the war on drugs. Reagan suggested that the Drug War had replaced the Cold War in importance. There was no doubt that a great deal of crime in the USA was drug-related (although drug-related deaths were far less than alcohol- and tobacco-related deaths).

Gun control

Although he had nearly been assassinated in 1981, Reagan opposed comprehensive legislation limiting the purchase and use of guns.

Women's rights

He was opposed to the Equal Rights Amendment and the cause of equal pay for jobs of comparable worth. Feminists were not really mollified by his naming the first woman justice to the Supreme Court, Sandra Day O'Connor. Opinion polls consistently reported a 'gender gap' in opinion on Reagan, who had less support among women that among men. Nevertheless, under Reagan more women entered the workforce than ever before.

Conclusion

Reagan proved himself to be what he claimed to be – a social conservative. But he did little to advance the social agenda of the Religious Right and disappointed some conservatives by not curtailing the core elements of the American welfare state.

Establish criteria

Below is a sample exam-style question which requires you to make a judgement. The key term in the question has been underlined. Defining the meaning of the key term can help you establish criteria that you can use to make a judgement.

Read the question, define the key term and then set out two or three criteria based on the key term, which you can use to reach and justify a judgement.

> Study Extracts 1 and 2. In the light of differing interpretations, how convincing do you find the view that President Reagan took little interest in social issues?

Definition:

_____

_____

Criteria to judge the extent to which President Reagan took little interest in social issues:

_____

_____

_____

_____

Historians have different views about the extent to which President Reagan actively involved his administration in social issues. Analyse and evaluate the extracts and use your own knowledge of the issues to explain your answer to the following question: How far do you agree with the view that President Reagan's social policies betrayed many Americans who were in need of help?

EXTRACT 1

From Gil Troy, Morning in America: How Ronald Reagan Invented the 1980s, *published in 2005*

Despite Reagan's traditionalism, his faith in individualism and his passive nature mostly furthered the various social and cultural revolutions he disliked. Even while believing they were choosing the old-fashioned way, Americans ratified many social changes by incorporating them into their lives. It was often an unhappy fit, sending indices of social pathology and individual misery soaring, yet Americans were acclimating to many of these problems. Increasingly 'the underclass', the 'teen-suicide epidemic', and 'family breakdown' were becoming familiar, static phenomena rather than crises to be solved. Overall, Reagan's 1980s accelerated the social solvents he blamed on the 1960s and 1970s. ... In the individualism he worshipped, the hypocrisy he embodied, and the politicisation of moral discourse he facilitated, Reagan further undermined the traditional collective mores he so proudly hailed. And as more of a compromiser than a revolutionary on social issues, he continued to institutionalise some of the changes. Most liberals were too busy demonizing Reaganite 'greed' and blindly defending the 1960s, big government, and anything Reagan opposed to notice, while most conservatives were simply too busy defending their hero just as blindly.

EXTRACT 2

From George Brown Tindall, America: A Narrative History, *published in 1988*

Feminists were offended by Reagan's opposition to the Equal Rights Amendment and abortion on demand, by the cuts in welfare which aggravated the 'feminisation' of poverty, and by his opposition to the cause of equal pay for jobs of comparable worth. ... Women in opposition were little mollified by his naming the first woman justice to the Supreme Court, Sandra Day O'Connor. Opinion polls consistently reported a 'gender gap' in opinion on Reagan, who had less support among women. Blacks and other minorities shared with women aggravation at the administration's limited support for affirmative action programmes in employment. In the administration itself the Civil Rights Commission reported in 1982 that only 8 percent of its appointments had gone to females and 8 percent to minorities, in contrast to 12 and 17 percent respectively under Carter. ... Funds for civil rights were among those targeted for reduction, and the Equal Employment Opportunity Commission's staff was sharply reduced.

The extent to which the presidency and US politics were revitalised under Reagan

Reagan's popularity

There is no doubt that few Americans had much confidence in Carter, Ford, Nixon or Johnson. Nor is there much doubt that Reagan was a popular president.

Reagan's character

Reagan was an amiable, charismatic and self-confident man. He came across well on TV. But those people who met him in the flesh invariably liked him too. So did many of his political enemies. He had a sense of style, which previous presidents lacked. Moreover, he had a clear (right-wing) American dream – a dream most Americans approved.

The 1984 election

In 1984, the Democrats chose Walter Mondale as their presidential candidate. Their vice presidential candidate was Geraldine Ferraro, the first female. The Republicans re-nominated Reagan and Bush with the slogan 'America is Back'. Mondale focused his attacks on Reagan's economic and foreign policies. Reagan's response was that most Americans were better off than they had been four years ago. He also stressed that the USA was not involved in conflict anywhere in the world. The main issue became that of taxation.

- Mondale said he would increase taxes to reduce the huge budget deficit.
- Reagan said there would be a tax increase only 'over my dead body'.

Reagan, who did not perform particularly well in the first TV debate, bounced back in the second. Responding to a question about the issue of age, 73-year old Reagan said: 'I'm not going to exploit for political purposes my opponent's youth and inexperience.'

Reagan's campaign was upbeat and successful. He won 58.9 per cent of the popular vote and every state except two. Except for black Americans, every section of the community preferred Reagan. He ran stronger than his party. The Republicans retained a slim majority in the Senate but remained a minority in the House.

Reagan's second term

Reagan remained popular. Nevertheless, in the 1986 **Congressional midterm elections** the Democrats won control of both houses of Congress.

The Iran-Contra affair

The **Irangate** scandal, which broke in 1986–87, might easily have led to Reagan's impeachment. In 1985, he had secretly authorised the sale of arms to Iran in order to secure the release of American hostages in the Middle East. CIA Director William Casey and Lieutenant Colonel Oliver North of the National Security Council established a system that diverted some of the money to purchase military supplies for the Contras – a right-wing who were trying to seize power in Nicaragua. This was in defiance of a 1984 Congressional ban. Reagan denied knowledge of the illegal proceedings but many believed that he had been fully aware of the situation. He was saved because:

- Congress had no wish to attack a popular president or re-open the wounds of Watergate.
- Vice Admiral John Poindexter and Lieutenant Colonel North were prepared to take the blame rather than implicate Reagan.
- most Americans were not greatly disturbed by the Irangate 'crime'.

Reagan's popularity

Success on the foreign policy stage and the USA's increasing prosperity ensured that Reagan had a popularity rating of 70 per cent in 1989 – higher than any president since Roosevelt. 'We meant to change a nation. And instead we changed a world. ... All in all, not bad, not bad at all', said Reagan in 1989.

There seems little doubt that he helped to restore the USA's confidence in itself and in its future. Reagan may not have been the most intelligent or hard-working president, but his letters reveal that he was more aware of events and more in control of them than his critics suggested. In many ways his impact was reminiscent of his early idol, Roosevelt. He was charismatic, delegated well, had clear goals and was a great communicator – believable because he himself believed what he said. He supplied the vision, voice and looks that helped restore the authority, dignity and prestige of the presidency after a long period of decline. He also did much to improve the USA's standing in the world. George Bush's election as president in 1988 owed much to Reagan's popularity.

Identify the interpretations

Below are a sample Section C exam question and the two accompanying extracts. The extracts offer different interpretations of the issue raised by the question. Read the extracts and underline the key interpretations in each extract.

In the light of differing interpretations how convincing do you find the view that Ronald Reagan was the most popular American president of the late-twentieth century? (Extract 1)

Study Extracts 1 and 2. Historians have different views about Reagan's political success. Analyse and evaluate the extracts and use your own knowledge of the issues to explain your answer to the following question: How far do you agree with the view that President Reagan was the USA's most popular president of the late-twentieth century?

EXTRACT 1

From Dinesh D'Souza, Ronald Reagan: How an Ordinary Man Became an Extraordinary Leader, *published in 1999*

Here was the son of the town drunk who grew up poor in the Midwest. Without any connections, he made his way to Hollywood and survived its cut-throat culture to become a major star. He ran as a right-wing candidate and was elected governor of California, the largest and one of the most progressive states in the country. He challenged the incumbent president, Gerald Ford, for the Republican nomination in 1976 and almost beat him. In 1980, he defeated Jimmy Carter to win the presidency in a landslide. He was re-elected in 1984 by one of the largest margins in history, losing only his opponent's home state of Minnesota and winning 525 electoral votes to Walter Mondale's 13. For eight consecutive years, the Gallup Poll pronounced him the most admired man in the country. When he left office, his approval rating was around 70 percent, the highest of any president in the modern era – higher than that of Eisenhower or Kennedy. He was one of the few presidents to bequeath the office to a hand-picked successor, George Bush, who was elected president in 1988 largely on the strength of Reagan's success. Moreover, Reagan was more than a mere occupant of the White House. Throughout the world, his name was identified with a coherent philosophy and outlook that people called 'Reaganism'. He thereby defined a whole era: the 1980s would be inconceivable without him.

EXTRACT 2

From Paul S. Boyer, Clifford E. Clark, Sandra Hawley, Joseph F. Kett, Andrew Rieser, The Enduring Vision: A History of the American People, *published in 2009*

After Nixon's disgrace, Ford's caretaker presidency and Carter's rocky tenure, Ronald Reagan's two terms restored a sense of stability and continuity to U.S. politics. Domestically, Reagan compiled a mixed record. Inflation eased and the economy improved after 1982. But the federal deficit soared and the administration largely ignored festering social issues, environmental concerns, and long-term economic problems. ... Reagan's critics dismissed his presidency as a time when self-interest trumped the public good, or, at best, as an interlude marked by nostalgia and drift rather than positive achievement. They noted how readily Reagan's celebration of individual freedom could morph into self-centred materialism. Apart from anti-Communism and flag-waving patriotism, they contended, Reagan offered few goals around which all Americans could rally ...

To his admirers, such criticism was itself mean-spirited, and beside the point. They credited Reagan for reasserting traditional values of self-reliance and free enterprise, criticising governmental excesses; and restoring national pride with his infectious optimism and patriotism. Reagan's militant anti-Communism spawned the Iran-Contra scandal, but also, his admirers believed, contributed mightily to America's victory in the Cold War – a victory whose full dimensions would become apparent after he left office.

How successful a president was Ronald Reagan?

Reagan's critics

Reagan had many critics at the time and has had many since. His critics tend to focus on his economic and social policies. They also emphasise that he was lucky.

Economic policies

Reagan's critics accept that he had some economic success, reducing both inflation and unemployment. However:

- Unemployment in the USA remained high.
- Under Reagan the rich got richer: it is not clear that their prosperity trickled down to the poor.
- The US economy experienced less growth than in the 1960s and 1970s.
- Under Reagan, the USA's national debt tripled.
- The USA became the world's biggest debtor nation.
- The USA's trade deficit increased massively: by 1990 it was over $150 billion a year.
- Foreign investors 'bought' up US real estate.

Social policies

Reagan did little to alleviate the USA's many social problems.

- He showed little sympathy for the various minority groups.
- He slashed welfare budgets.
- He did nothing to enhance female rights.
- Little was done to help drug addicts, the homeless, people suffering from AIDS or those suffering from mental illness.
- Although he stood for traditional family values, the traditional family continued to break down during his presidency. Divorce rates and unmarried teenage pregnancies increased.

A lucky president?

Arguably Reagan was essentially lucky.

- The fall in world oil prices came to his rescue economically.
- He was fortunate in foreign policy: the USSR was in difficulties by the 1980s.
- He managed to escape the Irangate scandal and a host of other scandals involving public officials whom he had appointed.

Essentially, he was the Teflon president on whom nothing stuck – but should have!

The case for Reagan

Reagan's admirers, of whom there were and have been many, tend to praise his political skill, his foreign policy success and his overall record.

Political (and economic) skill

- He achieved most of his aims.
- He reduced federal taxes.
- After 1983, the USA entered the longest peacetime period of uninterrupted economic growth in its history.
- He left the USA in a much stronger economic position than he found it.
- Whatever Reagan's rhetoric to the contrary, major New Deal and Great Society reforms remained rooted in the country's institutions.
- He boosted Americans' morale, giving them pride in themselves and in their country.
- He was genuinely popular. His popularity strengthened the institution of the presidency.

Foreign policy

He proved himself a confident and successful president on the world stage.

- He stood up to the USSR in his first term as president.
- He responded creatively to Gorbachev's overtures after 1985.
- The friendly relationship he established with Gorbachev helped bring an end to the Cold War.
- By 1988, the Cold War warrior had become the great peacemaker.
- He helped the USA win the Cold War.

A lucky president?

Undoubtedly Reagan had considerable luck as president. That is true of most successful presidents. The issue is to what extent he made his own luck. The fact that he had the reputation of being the Teflon president is testimony to his political skill. Nothing did stick! Admirers point out that Reagan was successful at virtually everything he did – sport commentating, acting, as governor of California (a difficult state for a right-wing Republican to govern) and as president. It seems unlikely that anyone could be so successful without having some extraordinary qualities.

Conclusion

Reagan was successful at selling his American dream to Americans. Yet in many respects he was a pragmatist. He never moved as far to the right as many on the left feared or as many of his followers hoped.

Add own knowledge

Read the following question and the accompanying extracts, then add detail from your own knowledge around the edges of both extracts. Draw links between the extracts and the details showing how they support or challenge the interpretations offered by the extracts. You can add knowledge that supports and challenges the extract. You can add new alternative arguments that challenge the interpretation offered by the extract.

> In the light of differing interpretations, how convincing do you find the view that President Reagan's presidency was more show that substance (Extract 1)?

Study Extracts 1 and 2. Historians have different views about the success of President Reagan's presidency. Analyse and evaluate the extracts and use your own knowledge of the issues to explain your answer to the following question: How far do you agree with the view that Reagan's presidency was successful with regard to both style and substance?

EXTRACT 1

From William H. Chafe, The Unfinished Journey: America Since World War II, *published in 1999*

At the end of the script, it was difficult to know where to place the critical emphasis. As Reagan supporter George Will noted, the president had produced an era of good feelings. Rhetoric had been essential to his presidency, because 'Reagan had intended his statecraft to be soulcraft'. But Will also acknowledged that Reagan's cheerful facade had been 'a narcotic, numbing the nation's senses about hazards just over the horizon'. By ignoring economic realities, disguising portents of disaster, and glossing over the rising presence of poverty, homelessness, and alienation, Reagan had bought time for the moment, from the harsh consequences that flowed from implementing his credo. He had played his part. But as *Newsweek* observed in its valedictory on the Administration, 'buried in the [economic] numbers was an almost Edwardian sense of decline, in industrial wealth, moral fibre and imperial sway'. ... The long Reagan spring had been a holiday from all that – from leaders who talked about malaise and sacrifice and what the country couldn't do. But his hour was passing, and at the dawn of [the next presidency], Americans for the first time in years were apprehensive about tomorrow again.

EXTRACT 2

From Glen Jeansonne, The 1980s and the Age of Reagan, *published in 2004*

Historians will argue the extent to which to credit or blame Reagan for the events that occurred on his watch. Liberals will find it difficult to credit him with the collapse of Communism and the prosperity of most of the 1980s. Some believe that Reagan's role as a shaper of history was no more intentional than that of Mrs O'Leary's cow, who kicked over a lantern and started the Chicago fire. Reagan accepted he would be judged partly on ideological terms because he was an ideological leader. He did not invent the idea that the federal government was too powerful and intrusive, nor did he demonise government in general: he had little negative to say about state and local governments. But he propelled the ideology of decentralisation along a route it was already travelling. He presented a set of ideas for which there was a demand and exerted charm and subtle pressure to enact them into law. Some of his most important changes did not involve laws at all, but moods. A relentless cheerleader, he urged Americans to conquer defeatism. Slow to anger, he was a gentle warrior – yet a warrior nonetheless. If Reagan was not a great president, neither was he a mediocre one. He came to office with a short agenda of big things and accomplished most of them. He demonstrated that common sense, sound judgement, and an uncanny intuition were more important than book learning.

The American Dream: Ronald Reagan's legacy

REVISED

Reagan's American dream

Reagan supported the traditional/conservative American dream – that of rugged individualism, patriotism and rejection of big government, which he perceived to be the problem rather than the solution to the USA's problems. In many ways Reagan personified the traditional dream: his life was very much one of 'rags to riches', achieved by his own skill, efforts and luck – as well as looks.

However, Reagan's dream was not supported by all Americans. Those on the left continued to support government intervention, ensuring assistance was provided to those who were less fortunate in society. Liberals believed that rich Americans – and US businesses – should be more heavily taxed to pay for spending which would help realise their progressive 'dream'.

What exactly was Reagan's legacy with regard to these opposing dreams – opposing dreams which had divided Americans through most of the twentieth century?

Reagan's political legacy

- Reagan seemed to have restored Americans' faith in the imperial presidency – a faith shattered by events in the 1960s and 1970s.

- In the 1980s, the USA shifted politically to the right. Reagan was able to hand power to his Vice President George Bush. However, the coalitions of economic and social conservatives that supported Reagan (and Bush) were fragile and did not guarantee continued Republican dominance – as Democrat Bill Clinton's success in 1992 proved.

- In some respects, Clinton – who had charm and charisma – continued Reagan's 'imperial' legacy. However, Clinton's 'dream' was more liberal, if not quite as progressive as many of his supporters hoped.

Reagan's economic legacy

During the 1980s, the USA moved from deep recession to economic prosperity. Nevertheless, critics feared that the tripling of the national debt – the result of tax cuts and massive defence spending – would have serious

repercussions. These fears proved to be ill-founded. US prosperity continued through the 1990s and into the early twenty-first century. Most Americans who wanted jobs had them, the stock market boomed and the nation had a budget surplus instead of a deficit. Reagan's pro-business policies created opportunities for the development of new technologies.

Reagan's social legacy

Economic policies benefited rich Americans. Despite claims to the contrary, there is not much evidence that their wealth trickled down to poorer Americans. Indeed, by 1989 the gulf between rich and poor had widened considerably. By the mid-1990s, the richest Americans owned 40 per cent of the USA's wealth. In the nation's most impoverished areas there was an increase in crime, violence and drug addiction.

During the 1980s, the face of the USA changed. A society that many had considered to be white and black became more diverse. The nation's Hispanic population grew in size and visibility. New immigrants from Asia arrived in large numbers: though still a small part of the population, they would play an increasingly important role in US society. During the Reagan years, the USA had thus become both more divided and more diverse.

Reagan's international legacy

Reagan's policies contributed considerably to the eventual break-up of the USSR. The result was that the USA was the world's lone superpower for two decades after 1989. How well it used its pre-eminence is a moot point.

Conclusion

In short, the impact and legacy of Reagan's presidency continue to divide historians just as contrary visions of the American dream had divided – and continue to divide – Americans.

Contrasting interpretations

Below are a sample Section C exam question and the accompanying extracts. The extracts offer different interpretations of the issue raised by the question. Identify the interpretation offered in each extract and complete the table below, indicating how far the extracts agree with each other, and explaining your answer.

	Extent of agreement	Justification
Extracts 1 and 2		

In the light of differing interpretations, how convincing do you find the view that Reagan was an able president who left a positive legacy?

Study Extracts 1 and 2. Historians have different views about President Reagan's legacy. Analyse and evaluate the extracts and use your knowledge of the issues to explain your answer to the following question.

How far do you agree with the view that the President Reagan left the USA with a clear and positive legacy?

EXTRACT 1

From Chester Pack, How do Historians Assess Ronald Reagan?, *published in 2001*

Reagan cared deeply about some issues and by the early 1960s, he had developed a clear, conservative philosophy, whose core was opposition to big government and the evils of communism, and that guided him throughout his political career. As president, he possessed an unshakeable certainty that his vision of the future would prevail – that tax cuts would produce prosperity, even as the recession of the early 1980s deepened; that communism would ultimately be relegated to 'the ash-heap of history,' as he predicted in 1982, even as the Cold War grew more intense. With remarkable effectiveness, Reagan set the political agenda for the 1980s. The visions that he considered most important, including tax reform, deregulation, reduction of social welfare programmes and increases in defence spending, dominated the politics of the decade. Reagan was brilliant and beguiling in rallying support for his programmes. But his public pronouncements, often laced with assertions of principle and moral certainty, masked a tactical flexibility that was one of his most notable assets as president. Reagan, despite his unconventional background, was hardly just an actor who happened to be good at saying his lines. He was an accomplished and resourceful politician.

EXTRACT 2

From Eric Foner, Give Me Liberty: An American History, *published in 2005*

Reagan's presidency revealed the contradictions at the heart of modern conservatism. Rhetorically, he sought to address the concerns of the Religious Right, advocating a 'return to spiritual values' as a way to strengthen traditional families and local communities. But in some ways, the Reagan Revolution undermined the very values and institutions conservatives held dear. Intended to discourage reliance on government handouts by rewarding honest work and business initiative, Reagan's policies inspired a speculative frenzy that enriched architects of corporate takeovers and investors in the stock market while leaving in their wake plant closures, job losses and devastated communities. Nothing proved more threatening to local traditions or family stability than de-industrialisation, insecurity about employment, and the relentless downward pressure on wages. Nothing did more to undermine a sense of common national purpose than the widening gap between rich and poor. Because of the Iran-Contra scandal and the enormous deficits the government had accumulated, Reagan left the presidency with his reputation somewhat tarnished.

Nonetheless, few figures have so successfully changed the landscape and language of politics. Reagan's vice president, George Bush, defeated Michael Dukakis, the governor of Massachusetts, in the 1988 election partly because Dukakis could not respond effectively to the charge that he was a 'liberal' – now a term of political abuse. Conservative assumptions about the virtues of the free market and the evils of 'big government' dominated the mass media and political debates.

Exam focus (A-level)

Below is a sample A-level essay. Read the question and the accompanying extracts, as well as the essay and the comments around it.

In the light of differing interpretations, how convincing do you find the view that President Reagan restored economic prosperity to the United States?

EXTRACT 1

From William H. Chafe, The Unfinished Journey: America Since World War II, *published in 1999*

As if the chaos in national security affairs were not enough, the economy began to display some of the long-term consequences of Reagan's tax and fiscal policies. Despite constant warnings that massive increases in military expenditures would generate excessive deficits, Reagan refused to propose new taxes and continued to act as if there were no problem. Although he systematically blamed Congress for its role in creating deficits, he seemed congenitally incapable of acknowledging that he was to blame for 95 percent of the problem, since it was his budgets that created the dilemma. The Reagan tax cuts, combined with a 41 percent real increase in the defence budget, caused the federal deficit to soar from $90 billion in 1982 to $283 billion in 1986 – nearly ten times the highest deficit under any previous president. To finance the debt, America had to borrow, raising interest rates to attract capital. What that did, in turn, was to generate a flow of foreign money into America, which then caused the value of the dollar to rise dramatically, out of all proportion to its true worth. As the dollar skyrocketed, imports became cheaper – forcing many American industries either to relocate to third-world countries or go out of business – and the nation's trade imbalance also went haywire, since foreign markets could not afford to buy American goods at the inflated dollar value that now prevailed.

EXTRACT 2

From Martin Anderson, Revolution *(1988)*

President Reagan set spending records right and left. Holding to his many pledges over the years to strengthen social security, the health care system, and welfare, and to build up our national defences, he directed massive increases in social welfare and welfare spending and for national defence. That's where most of the money went.

There were other things that happened during this unprecedented economic expansion. Thrashing the conventional wisdom of economics, inflation plummeted as the economy rolled on. From high double digits in 1980, inflation dropped to single digits and stayed there. Interest rates dropped. And the stock market boomed, setting new historical highs nearly every week, it seemed, in the optimistic summer of 1987 ...

Most of what we accomplished in this decade was possible because of economic growth, the main fuel for the spending engine, but we also had a little help from others. From 1980 through to the end of 1987, President Reagan borrowed $1 for every $5 he spent, so that the national debt increased by $1.2 trillion dollars. The United States was one of the best credit risks in the world, people pressed money on us, and we obliged, borrowing easily, quickly and almost guiltlessly ... Borrowing the trillion dollars may have been the smartest thing we ever did.

Extract 1 argues that Reagan's economic policies were a disaster for the United States' economy. It lays the blame directly at Reagan's door, accusing him of being 'congenitally incapable' of acknowledging his responsibility for the USA's burgeoning budget deficit – the crux of the country's economic problem. Extract 2, by contrast, provides a very upbeat view of the American economy by the end of Reagan's 'watch'. It praises Reagan for his massive spending, claiming that this led to economic expansion. It regards government borrowing as a positive – 'the smartest thing we ever did'. The debate over Reagan's Keynesian-esque economic policies is crucial to the way his presidency is assessed. It is also crucial to the way American governments have operated since 1988. Perhaps

This essay opens by demonstrating a clear understanding of the extracts and provides a very clear indication of how the essay is likely to – controversially – proceed.

the crucial consideration is that the doom and gloom predictions of many of Reagan's contemporaries and of historians like William Chafe (in Extract 1) never came to pass. The United States economy boomed after 1983 and continued to boom for most of the 1990s. This suggests that 'Reaganomics' worked. Reagan restored economic prosperity to the USA and he did so by expanding the economy rather.

There is general consensus among historians that Reagan inherited a deplorable economic situation in 1981. His predecessors – Nixon, Ford and Carter – had failed to tackle the problem of 'stagflation' – high inflation and high unemployment. Reagan's solution was to cut taxes and to encourage American business. He claimed that this would encourage enterprise which would eventually bring in more – not less – revenue. He did not seem particularly concerned about government expenditure. He was committed to cutting some aspects of welfare spending. But he was totally committed to increasing government spending on defence: 'defence is not a budget item ... you spend what you need'. His critics thought his policies were irresponsible. John Anderson, the independent candidate in 1980, said that Reagan's economic plans would have to be done with 'blue smoke and mirrors'. Perhaps there was some truth in this. The conjuring trick was not worrying about the government deficit. Right-wing Reagan essentially adopted left-wing Keynesian economic policies – a fact not admitted by either his liberal opponents or his conservative admirers. And as Extract 2 argues, Keynesian magic worked. The US economy expanded big time after 1983 and economic growth fuelled economic prosperity.

Extract 1 expresses concern over Reagan's desire to cut taxes and massively increase military expenditure. This would, inevitably, increase the federal budget deficit. And it did – to $283 billion in 1986. Extract 1 bemoans this, the highest deficit under any previous president. Reagan's administration had to borrow to cover their debt. It did so by raising interest rates to attract capital, from both home and abroad. Extract 1 implies that the USA sold its soul to foreign capitalists. It claims that Reagan's policies resulted in the dollar 'skyrocketing' in value with the result that imports from abroad became cheaper and it was harder for American firms to sell goods abroad. The result, Extract 1 claims, was disastrous. American businesses either relocated to third-world countries or went bankrupt. Meanwhile, the US balance of trade imbalance went 'haywire' and the USA became the world's largest debtor nation. There is some truth in Extract 1's description of what happened economically in the 1980s. Unfortunately for Extract 1's prognosis – and very fortunately for the American economy – there was no economic disaster. Extract 1 concentrates on minutia. It does not take into account the big picture of what was happening.

Extract 2 does grasp the big picture. As a result of high interest rates initially and a sharp fall in oil prices (sheer luck on Reagan's part but successful presidents invariably are lucky) inflation did fall dramatically (allowing interest rates to fall). The stock market boomed and the economy boomed. Between November 1982 and November 1987 more wealth and services were produced than any like period in American history. Some 15 million new jobs were created – the greatest five-year employment growth in US history. By 1988 the USA was producing 65 per cent a year more than when Carter left office in January 1981. Extract 2 accepts that the US 'did have a little help from others'. But it sees foreign investment as a good thing rather than a bad. The fact that so many foreigners were prepared to invest in the USA was itself evidence that the USA was an excellent credit risk.

Reagan, in part, made good on his promise to cut taxes. The Economic Recovery Act of 1981 reduced the highest tax rates to 28 per cent and included across-the-board tax reductions of 25 per cent. The Tax Reform Act of 1986 greatly simplified the entire tax structure. Extract 1 is critical of Reagan's tax policy, claiming it fuelled the federal deficit.

This meaty paragraph integrates issues raised by the extracts with those from own knowledge. The fact that it does not sit on the fence is not a problem. It presents a clear, evaluative argument and goes down the road indicated in the introductory paragraph.

This paragraph interprets Extract 1 with confidence. The last three sentences are very good – putting the extract firmly in its place, at least in the eyes of the candidate.

Good reference to Extract 2's main argument. It integrates issues raised by the extract with those from own knowledge and does so most effectively.

However, it does not point out that Reagan was better with 'blue smoke' and 'mirrors' than many of his critics suggest. He did surreptitiously raise taxes in 1982, largely by closing tax loopholes. Even with regard to one of his most cherished principles, Reagan was prepared to be pragmatic.

A short but interesting paragraph, which focuses on one of Extract 1's claims. Good reference back to 'smoke and mirrors'.

Extract 1 is also unfair with regard to blaming the federal deficit solely on Reagan's defence spending. In reality, the federal government under Reagan continued to spend huge sums on social security, Medicare and health. In 1980, the US spent $40 billion a year more on these programmes than on national defence. By 1988, after the largest peacetime military spending increase in US history, the USA was still spending $37 billion a year more on social security, Medicare and health programmes than on national defence.

Another attack on Extract 1, this time on Reagan's actual spending. Very good own knowledge displayed.

In conclusion, Reagan's economic spending undoubtedly did result in a huge increase in the USA's national debt. Extract 1 condemns him for this, implying that it damaged the US economy at the time and had fearsome consequences for the future. Extract 1 is wrong on both scores. Reaganomics resulted in an economic boom from late 1982 to 1988. The deficit also had very little impact on the USA's future economic development. Indeed, Democrat President Bill Clinton generally adopted 'Reaganomic' principles during his two terms as president. Extract 2, which regards Reagan's economic policies positively, provides a far more persuasive overview of 'Reaganomics' in action. Reagan did spend the USA out of recession as many wanted Roosevelt to do in the 1930s. Roosevelt did not go as far as down the Keynesian road as Reagan – a huge supporter of Roosevelt's New Deal policies in the 1930s. The result was that Reagan had far more economic success than Roosevelt (pre-1941). Economic growth was the key to economic prosperity as Extract 2 recognises. And economic growth and prosperity is what Reagan succeeded in bringing about.

The conclusion finishes the sustained evaluative argument developed across the essay. Yes, the essay is controversial, but it supports its argument with excellent factual knowledge and understanding.

This essay achieves a mark in Level 5 as it interprets both extracts with confidence and clearly understands the basis of the interpretations offered by both extracts. It also integrates issues raised by the extracts with those from own knowledge and presents a sustained evaluative argument (albeit one which could be challenged!), reaching a fully substantiated judgement on the interpretations of both extracts.

Reverse engineering

The best essays are based on careful plans. Read the essay and the examiner's comments and try to work out the general points of the plan used to write the essay. Also look at how the two extracts are used in the answer. Once you have done this, note down the specific examples used to support each general point.

For those taking the AS exam, an example Section C question and model answer can be found on www.hoddereducation.co.uk/myrevisionnotes.

Glossary

14th Amendment This declared that all persons born or naturalised in the United States were citizens of the USA. It asserted that no state could abridge the privileges and immunities of US citizens or deprive any person of life, liberty or property without due process of law, or deny any citizen the equal protection of the laws. Essentially, it guaranteed civil rights for all Americans.

15th Amendment This states that the right to vote should not be denied on account of race, colour or previous condition of servitude.

Administration This is the American term for government. Kennedy's administration was Kennedy's government team.

Affirmative action Giving disadvantaged minorities extra opportunities (even if others were better qualified) in education and employment in order to compensate for previous unfair treatment.

American dream Belief that the nature of US society enables an individual to fulfil his or her potential, especially through wealth.

Anarchist A person whose ideal of society is one without a government of any kind: extreme anarchists might support the use of terrorism to bring this about.

Arab-Israeli War A war in the Middle East that began in 1973 when Egypt and Syria attacked Israel. Israel won.

Attorney general Head of the Justice Department in the federal government.

Baby boom Post-Second World War population boom following the servicemen's return home.

Balance of trade deficit When the value of the goods imported by a nation exceeds the value of the goods exported.

Black Panthers A group of militant black activists who used revolutionary language, openly carried guns and distributed free meals to the ghetto poor.

Brain Trust The name given to President Roosevelt's unofficial advisers, many of whom were academics, lawyers and journalists.

Budget deficit When a government's spending exceeds its income.

Bussing Supreme Court rulings on integrated education meant some white children were sent by bus to black schools and vice versa.

Cash and carry In 1939 the USA agreed to sell arms to Britain provided Britain paid for the weapons in cash and transported them in British ships.

Chapters Local branches of an association.

Checkers speech This speech refers to Richard Nixon's speech in 1952 when he used TV (successfully) to defend his reputation. In the speech he cleverly referred to his daughter's dog, Checkers.

CIA The Central Intelligence Agency was set up in 1947 to monitor Communist threats early in the Cold War.

Civil War The American Civil War, fought between the North and South, took place between 1861 and 1865.

Cold War The struggle between the capitalist USA and the Communist Soviet Union.

Communist A believer in economic equality brought about by revolutionary redistribution of wealth, usually orchestrated by the government.

Congress The US equivalent of Britain's Parliament, it consists of the House of Representatives and the Senate. Each US state selects two senators and a number of House Congressmen proportionate to its population.

Congressional midterm elections Congressional elections are held every two years: thus, elections are held along with the president's election and in the middle of the president's term.

Consciousness-raising meetings Procedures adopted by radical feminists to raise awareness of women's rights.

Consumerism Great interest in acquiring consumer goods such as cars and kitchen appliances.

Counterculture An alternative lifestyle to the dominant culture: in the case of 1960s' America, the 'drop-out' mentality as compared to the dominant, materialistic hard-working culture of the students' parents.

Crack A highly addictive form of cocaine.

Cuban Missile Crisis The USSR's attempt to establish nuclear missile sites in Cuba in 1962 led to a crisis between the USSR and the USA which threatened to spark a nuclear war.

De facto segregation Black and white people segregated in residential areas and some other public places in practice if not in law.

Deep South States such as Mississippi, Alabama and Georgia where segregation and racism were most deeply entrenched.

Democrat A member of one of the two main political parties. In comparison to Republicans, Democrats tend to be more supportive of government intervention and more on the left of the political spectrum.

Devaluation/devalued currency This is a reduction in the value internationally of a country's currency, usually as a result of the lowering of the exchange rate with other currencies.

Disfranchisement Denied the right to vote.

Electoral College This is the body which actually elects the American president. Each state, depending on its population size, sends a specific number of Electoral College voters to elect the president.

Evangelical A more enthusiastic type of Protestant who often takes the Bible very literally.

Executive powers The US Constitution gives the president various powers. They can be challenged by state or federal judges and by Congress.

FBI The Federal Bureau of Investigation – a police force which is allowed to cross state boundaries.

Federal government The national or federal government, based in Washington DC, consists of the president, Congress (which makes laws) and the Supreme Court (which interprets laws).

Feminist An advocate of equal political, social, economic and legal rights for women.

Food stamp programmes First used during the Great Depression, they were made permanent by the Food Stamp Act (1964). Poor people present stamps provided by the government for food.

Fourteen points These were President Wilson's ideas which he hoped would be the basis of a fair and lasting peace with Germany.

Ghetto An area inhabited mostly or solely by (usually poor) members of a particular ethnicity or nationality.

GI Bill This allowed returning US servicemen the opportunity to go to university or college free of charge.

GNP A country's gross national product is the aggregate value of goods and services produced in that country.

Great Depression Starting with the 1929 Wall Street Crash, the US economy was characterised by unprecedented unemployment in the early 1930s.

Great Migration The Northward movement of Southern blacks during the twentieth century.

Great Society President Johnson's plan to create an American society free from racism and poverty which were particularly prevalent in the urban ghettos.

Harlem New York City's main black area.

Hippies Young people, often students, who in the 1960s rejected the beliefs and fashions of the older generation and favoured free love and drugs.

House of Representatives One of the two congressional chambers. Each state elects a number of congressmen proportional to its population to the House every two years.

Impeachment Under the US Constitution, Congress has the power to bring an errant president to trial, to impeach him.

Imperial presidency During the Cold War, presidential power increased so much that some commentators thought the president was becoming like an emperor – hence 'imperial'.

Inaugural address A speech made by the president or state governor after he has been sworn into office.

Indo-China The region which today comprises Vietnam, Cambodia and Laos. This area had once been ruled by France.

Irangate/Iran-Contra scandal This arose in 1986. Members of Reagan's administration, without Congressional approval, sold arms to Iran to secure the release of hostages. The money was used to provide weapons for the Nicaraguan Contras who were fighting against a left-wing Nicaraguan government.

Iran hostage crisis In 1979 Iranian revolutionaries seized the US embassy in Tehran and took 60 American hostages. They held them until 1980.

Isolationism Long-standing US foreign policy tradition whereby the US avoids foreign entanglements.

Keynesian economics Keynes was a British economist who claimed that governments should be prepared to overspend, if necessary, to put nations on the road to economic recovery.

Laissez-faire A general principle of non-interference.

League of Nations A body similar to the United Nations, set up after 1919 to try and preserve world peace.

Lend-lease A program under which the US supplied Allied nations with food, oil and materiel between 1941 and 1945.

Lynching Unlawful killing (usually by hanging).

Materialism Excessive preoccupation with material goods and consumerism.

McCarthyism Anti-Communist hysteria associated with Senator McCarthy.

Medicare Introduced by President Johnson in 1965, this provided federally funded health insurance for over-65s and those with disabilities.

National Guard State reserves that are raised by state governors or the president during an emergency.

NATO The treaty setting up the North Atlantic Treaty Organisation was signed in April 1949. It initially comprised the USA, Canada, Britain, France, Belgium, Luxembourg, Holland, Norway, Italy, Portugal, Iceland and Denmark.

New Deal Roosevelt's plan to get the USA out of Depression.

Per capita For each person.

Permissive society The name given to the type of liberal society resulting from the sexually and socially liberating 1960s.

Plessy v Ferguson ruling (1896) This Supreme Court decision had accepted segregation provided facilities for both black and white were equal.

Religious Right Influential late 1970s movement which arose in reaction to the liberalism and counterculture of the 1960s.

Republican A member of one of the two main political parties. Its members are usually more conservative than Democrats and generally opposed to federal government intervention.

Rosie the Riveter Rosie was the name of a fictitious woman, used by government posters, to encourage women to take up war work in the USA between 1941 and 1945.

Senate One of the two chambers of Congress. Two senators are elected from each state. Senators sit for six years before re-election.

Service industries Businesses that serve customers but are not involved in manufacturing, for example restaurants and shops.

Sharecroppers Tenant farmers who give a share of their crops produced to the landowner as rent.

Sit-ins When protestors sat in the 'wrong' seats in restaurants and refused to move, causing the establishment to lose custom and then – hopefully – desegregate.

Sovereignty Ultimate power.

Speakeasy A place selling illegal alcohol in the age of Prohibition.

Stagflation A period of high inflation combined with high unemployment and slow economic growth.

Supreme Court This body issues rulings on whether or not laws and actions are in line with the Constitution.

Syndicalist A person who supports the idea of putting the means of production in the hands of unions of workers.

Third American Revolution The name sometimes given to the New Deal. The first Revolution was the War of American Independence; the second was the American Civil War.

Third World This refers to the new countries, mainly in Africa and Asia, which emerged in the 1950s and 1960s as the old European empires collapsed.

Uppity A term used by southern whites in reference to troublesome blacks who 'did not know their place'.

USSR The Union of Soviet Socialist Republics – or Soviet Union.

Wall Street The financial centre of the USA.

Western Hemisphere The North and South American continents.

White flight The post-1945 exodus of white Americans from inner-city areas which were then left to minorities, usually blacks or Hispanics.

Witch hunt The searching out and persecuting of political opponents.

Key figures

Jimmy Carter (1924–) Born in Georgia, his father was a successful peanut farmer. A Democrat, Carter served as Governor of Georgia (1970–74). Against the odds, he won the 1976 election. He is generally considered an ineffective president. He had a poor legislative record. While he helped broker peace between Egypt and Israel, he had few other foreign policy successes. He dealt unsuccessfully with the Iranian hostage situation in 1979–80 and was defeated by Reagan in 1980.

Fidel Castro (1926–2016) Castro was the Communist dictator of Cuba for most of the late twentieth century.

Calvin Coolidge (1872–1933) Elected Republican governor of Massachusetts in 1918, 'Cal' Coolidge won national attention by using state troops against striking Boston police in 1919. Elected vice president in 1920, he became president when Warren Harding died in 1923. Coolidge won election in his own right in 1924. In office 'Silent Cal' said and did little but symbolised the virtues of honesty and sober practicality. He was committed to freeing business from government restraints.

Dwight D. Eisenhower (1890–1969) Raised in Kansas, Eisenhower attended West Point military academy (1911–15). From 1942–45 he commanded US forces in Europe, leading the invasion of France in 1944. In 1950 he became NATO commander. Appointed Republican presidential candidate in 1952, he won the election and was re-elected in 1956. Although he suffered from ill health, he proved himself a strong and generally successful president.

Betty Friedan (1921–2006) Friedan, a graduate and housewife, gained a national reputation for her best-selling book *The Feminine Mystique*. This is usually seen as the book which launched the women's rights movement. She went on to become a founder and first president of the National Organisation for Women.

Mahatma Gandhi (1869–1948) Gandhi had led resistance to British rule in India. Rather than supporting violence, he had used mass disobedience campaigns.

Herbert Hoover (1874–1964) Orphaned at the age of nine, Hoover, a successful engineer, became a self-made millionaire. During the First World War he achieved world stature for co-ordinating relief for Belgium. An active Republican secretary of commerce in the 1920s, he was elected president in 1928. He thus had to face the Great Depression. His critics said he did not do enough to help those Americans most in need. In reality, his administration took a great deal of action. He received little credit and was easily defeated by Roosevelt in 1932.

Lyndon Baines Johnson (1908–73) Born in Texas, Johnson spent his life in public service. A congressman from 1937–49, he became a senator in 1949 and vice president in 1961. Following Kennedy's assassination, he became president. Master of the American legislative process, he was determined to push through his Great Society programme, which he hoped would end poverty. But from 1965 he was increasingly focused on the Vietnam War. As the war went badly, he became increasingly unpopular and did not stand for re-election in 1968.

John F. Kennedy (1917–63) Born into a very wealthy family, Kennedy's political career was boosted by his father's wealth and influence. After an undistinguished career in Congress, he became Democratic presidential candidate in 1960, defeating Nixon to become president. Youthful and charismatic, he was a good television performer and brought some style and glamour to the White House. His main interest was foreign affairs and he was determined to stand up to the Soviet Union. The 1962 Cuban missile crisis took the world to the brink of nuclear war. Kennedy was assassinated in Dallas in 1963.

Martin Luther King (1929–68) Born into a relatively prosperous family in Atlanta, King was well educated and became a pastor in Montgomery where he became prominent in the 1955–56 bus boycott. In 1957 he established SCLC and was generally recognised as one of the main leaders of the civil rights movement in the late 1950s and early 1960s. In 1963 he organised the Birmingham campaign against segregation and gave his great 'I have a dream' speech during a march on Washington. His northern campaign after 1965 was less successful than his work in the South. He was assassinated in 1968 by James Earl Ray.

Malcolm X (1925–65) Born with the name Malcolm Little in Nebraska, he moved to Boston in 1941. In 1946, he was sentenced to ten years' imprisonment for drug dealing and theft. In prison he joined the Nation of Islam and on his release in 1952, adopting the name Malcolm X, he became one of the Nation's main recruiters and speakers. He proclaimed black separatism. Splitting from the Nation in 1964, he was assassinated by Nation gunmen in 1965.

Richard Nixon (1913–94) Born to a struggling California family, Nixon practised law before becoming a major Republican politician. He gained national fame through his work in pursuit of

Communists (1947–52). He became Eisenhower's vice president in 1952. Defeated by Kennedy in 1960, Nixon made an amazing political comeback and was elected president in 1968 and re-elected in 1972. He slowly ended the Vietnam War but had little success on the economic front. The Watergate scandal brought about his downfall. Threatened with impeachment, he resigned as president in 1974.

Rosa Parks (1913–2005) Born in Montgomery, she married Raymond Parks, a founder member of Montgomery's NAACP. She became an active NAACP member after 1942. In 1955, she was arrested for refusing to give up her seat on a bus, an action that began the Montgomery bus boycott. Branded a troublemaker, she and her husband lost their jobs and moved to Detroit in 1957.

Ronald Reagan (1911–2004) Born in Illinois, Reagan was a very successful sports commentator, Hollywood screen actor and television star. Once a left winger, he became a conservative Republican in the late 1940s. From 1967–74 he served two terms as governor of California. Known as the 'great communicator', he appealed to voters with his easy charm and his repeated attacks on big government and liberals. He won the Republican nomination in 1980 (he just failed in 1976) and went on to win the

election. He was re-elected in 1984. Under-estimated by many people at the time, he is now generally regarded as a successful president who improved the economic situation in America, contributed greatly to the end of the Cold War and restored the prestige of the presidency.

Franklin Delano Roosevelt (1882–1945) Born into a wealthy family in New York State, he married Eleanor Roosevelt in 1905. In 1913, he became assistant secretary of the navy. His political career seemed to be at an end when he was struck down by polio in 1921; he was unable to walk unaided thereafter. But in 1928 he became governor of New York. Elected Democratic president in 1932, he remained president until his death. His New Deal measures helped the USA out of the Depression and he proved himself a very effective war leader after 1941.

Harry Truman (1884–1972) Born on a Missouri farm, he served successfully in the First World War. He was elected senator for Missouri in 1935. Elected as Roosevelt's vice presidential running mate in 1944, he became president on Roosevelt's death in 1945. He took the decision to drop atomic bombs on Japan. In 1947 he announced that the USA would do its best to contain Communism. He won the 1948 election and took the USA into the Korean War in 1950.

Timeline

1917	USA entered the First World War against Germany
1918	President Wilson announced his Fourteen Points
	End of the First World War
1919	Volstead Act (Prohibition introduced)
1919–20	USA rejected the League of Nations
	Red Scare
1920	Harding elected president
1923	Death of Harding
	Coolidge became president
1924	Coolidge elected president
1927	Babe Ruth hit 60 home runs in one year
1928	Hoover elected president
1929	Wall Street Crash
	Start of Great Depression
1932	Roosevelt elected president
1933	The Hundred Days
1935	Social Security Act
	Neutrality Act
1936	Roosevelt re-elected president
1937	Supreme Court 'packing' fight
1939	Start of Second World War
1940	Roosevelt re-elected president for a third term: a record
1941	USA gave Lend-Lease aid to the Allies
	Japanese attack on Pearl Harbor
	The USA entered the Second World War
1944	Roosevelt re-elected president for a record fourth term:
1945	Death of Roosevelt
	Truman became president
	Atomic bombs dropped on Hiroshima and Nagasaki
	End of Second World War
1947	Truman Doctrine highlighted the need to contain Communism
	Marshall Aid promised to Europe
1948	Truman elected president
1950	Senator McCarthy declared there were Communists in the State Department
	Start of Korean War
1952	Eisenhower elected president
1953	End of Korean War
1954	Army-McCarthy hearings
	Brown v Board of Education, Topeka decision

1955–56	Montgomery bus boycott
1956	Eisenhower re-elected
1957	Civil Rights Act
	Little Rock, Arkansas crisis
1960	Sit-in movement began in Greensboro
	Kennedy elected president
1961	Freedom Rides
1963	*The Feminine Mystique* published
	Civil Rights March on Washington
	Kennedy assassinated
	Johnson became president
1964	Start of summer riots in black ghettos
	Civil Rights Act
	Johnson elected president
1965	Assassination of Malcolm X
	Johnson launched his Great Society programme
	Medicare and Medicaid introduced
	Voting Rights Act
1966	National Organisation of Women established
	Black Panthers established
1968	Assassination of Martin Luther King
	Serious riots in the black ghettos
	Nixon elected president
1969	Woodstock Festival for Music and Peace
	Neil Armstrong became the first man on the moon
1972	Nixon re-elected
1973	Vietnam Peace agreement
	Arab oil embargo
1973–74	The Watergate affair
1974	Nixon resigned
	Ford became president
1975	South Vietnam fell to Communists
1976	Carter elected president
1979	Iran took 60 Americans hostage
1980	Reagan became president
1981	Reagan tax cuts
1984	Reagan re-elected president
1986	Tax reform act
1986	Iran-Contra affair
1988	Bush elected president

Mark scheme

AO1 mark scheme

REVISED ☐

- **Analytical focus**
- **Accurate detail**
- **Supported judgement**
- Argument and structure

AS Marks		A-level Marks
1–4	**Level 1** ● Simplistic, limited focus ● Limited detail, limited accuracy ● No judgement or asserted judgement ● **Limited organisation, no argument**	1–3
5–10	**Level 2** ● Descriptive, implicit focus ● Limited detail, mostly accurate ● Judgement with limited support ● **Basic organisation, limited argument**	4–7
11–16	**Level 3** ● Some analysis, clear focus (may be descriptive in places) ● Some detail, mostly accurate ● Judgement with some support, based on implicit criteria ● **Some organisation, the argument is broadly clear**	8–12
17–20	**Level 4** ● Clear analysis, clear focus (may be uneven) ● Sufficient detail, mostly accurate ● Judgement with some support, based on valid criteria ● **Generally well organised, logical argument (may lack precision)**	13–16
	Level 5 ● Sustained analysis, clear focus ● Sufficient accurate detail, fully answers the question ● Judgement with full support, based on valid criteria (considers relative significance) ● **Well organised, logical argument communicated with precision**	17–20

AO3 mark scheme

- **Interpretation and analysis of the extracts**
- **Knowledge of issues related to the debate**
- **Evaluation of the interpretations**

AS Marks		A-level Marks
1–4	**Level 1** ● Limited comprehension of the extracts demonstrated through selecting material ● Some relevant knowledge, with limited links to the extracts ● Judgement has little or no support	1–3
5–10	**Level 2** ● Some understanding of the extracts demonstrated by describing some of their relevant points ● Relevant knowledge added to expand on details in the extracts ● Judgement relates to the general issue rather than the specific view in the question, with limited support	4–7
11–16	**Level 3** ● Understanding of the extracts demonstrated through selecting and explaining some of their key points ● Relevant knowledge of the debate links to or expands some of the views given in the extracts ● Judgement relates to some key points made by the extracts, with some support	8–12
17–20	**Level 4** ● Understanding of the extracts demonstrated through analysis of their interpretations, and a comparison of the extracts ● Relevant knowledge of the debate integrated with issues raised by the extracts. Most of the relevant aspects of the debate are discussed – although some may lack depth ● Judgement relates to the interpretations of the extracts and is supported by a discussion of the evidence and interpretations of the extracts	13–16
	Level 5 ● Interpretation of the extracts demonstrated through a confident and discriminating analysis of their interpretations, clearly understanding the basis of both their arguments ● Relevant knowledge of the debate integrated in a discussion of the evidence and arguments presented by the extracts ● Judgement relates to the interpretations of the extracts and is supported by a sustained evaluative argument regarding the evidence and interpretations of the extracts	17–20